TOWARDS PEACE

TOWARDS PEACE

DR. RAVINDRA KUMAR

GYAN PUBLISHING HOUSE
NEW DELHI-110002

Towards Peace

Rs. 540

ISBN:81-212-0920-X

Published in 2007 in India by
Gyan Publishing House
5, Ansari Road, Darya Ganj,
New Delhi-110002
Phones : 23282060, 23261060
Fax : 011-23285914
E-mail : books@ gyanbooks.com
Website: www.gyanbooks.com

Lassertype Setting by: Rudra Computer Graphics
Printed at : Salasar Imaging System, Delhi

Contents

Self-Atterance

I had a chance to write articles on various topics related to Religion, Philosophy, Culture, Civilization and some other subjects during the last eleven years [1995-2006]. Other subjects have been Armament, Militarization, Peace and Peace-Education. I have attempted to make critical analysis of the above-mentioned subjects according to my knowledge or whatever experience I have gained in relation to them.

I believe that culture or civilization, religion or philosophy all call upon the humanity to adopt peace. They all contribute to the attainment of peace, which is essential for human life. All incarnations, messengers, great men and saints ultimately declared peace to be the goal of human life. Subsequently, they showed practical ways of gaining it. Mahatma Gandhi visualized formation of a fearless world. He adopted truth and non-violence as basis towards this end. These are ultimately the means to take human world to prosperity and peace. This is the reason that the basis of all my above-mentioned articles had been peace.

In context of these articles, my friends in India and abroad have been constantly pressurizing me to have them published in a book form. My publishers' desire has also been to have them published. Resultantly, I desisted myself from many other activities and gave these articles a form of a manuscript. While doing so, I divided it into four parts:

- Caste and Class;
- Culture and Civilization;
- Religion and Philosophy; and
- Miscellaneous.

In part first two articles on Caste System, which has always disintegrated our society and is responsible for creating state of inequality in it, have been included.

In second part there are some articles related to Culture and Civilization. They contain topics like Indian Culture: A Perspective, Indian Culture and Social Life, Impact of Indian Culture upon Thai Life, Indian Civilization at the Close of Twentieth Century and Fundamental Principles of Civilization.

Good or welfare – oriented religion and good order, both are always related to human prosperity and peace. This is the reason that central point of all religious communities, including Hinduism and Buddhism, has been human prosperity and ultimately peace. Articles incorporated in part third in which one is based on ever green teachings of Lord Buddha, lead human beings towards prosperity and peace, along with a good order to gain them.

All other articles have been incorporated in the last – that is fourth part. This is the miscellaneous section. In it, some articles which are, too, based upon my experiences and memories, related to subjects like Nuclear-Religious Conflicts and Peace in South Asia, For the Establishment of Fearless and Peaceful World, India and the Asian Values, Problem before Society and Nation and Obligations of

Intelligentsia, Indian View of Peace, and India and the World: With Special Reference to Twenty-First Century.

So divided in 4 parts, the manuscript has been entitled 'Towards Peace '. It is possible, and it is a hope that readers in general and those with subject – interest shall be getting some useful information after it is published.

I am grateful to all those who have extended their assistance in preparation of this manuscript. I am especially thankful to Mr. Sachin Bathla, Mrs. Megha Arora and Mr. Sachin Arora for reading the manuscript before sending it for publication.

Ravindra Kumar

A

CASTE AND CLASS

1. Religion and Caste

It is an irony that we try to intermingle caste system with religion. It is also regrettable that we affix seal of religion on caste system and thereby we intentionally keep ourselves away from true religion. The truth happens to be that religion can never be, in any way,[1] a helping hand to a system like caste system that is identified, as a factor of disintegration in society. Not only this, the aims and objects of any religious community are as distant from the caste system as the earth is away from the sun.

Religion had originated with man's march on this earth. It can be put in this way - when the Creator sent man on earth in accordance with His action, He also sent religion along with him. As such, man and religion came to earth simultaneously. There is also a purpose behind the fact that both came together. A question is natural about purpose. We shall easily comprehend it if we comprehend the meaning of religion in very simple terms.

As I hold, religion signifies adoption. What is to be adopted? As always, my reply is ***'goodness'*** or ***'niceness'***. As such, religion consists in adopting goodness. It is only goodness owing to presence of which man could sustain his existence. He gradually developed non-violence and then adopted a path of mutual co-operation.

Man came to earth with action in nature. In such a situation, man might have ended his existence in case religion was not with him. ...But, he not only maintained his existence, but also marched forward on the path of progress. This is the reason that human being and religion came together. When? Or what is the span of time in this respect? This can be a topic for research. ...However, both originated and grew up simultaneously.

We should know the meaning of religion in simple terms. It is clear that it stands for existence and welfare of man. Its basis is cooperation, affection and unity. It propagated message of ***'Live and Let Live'.*** In this regard, any action, contrary to the spirit of cooperation, affection or unity cannot be religious. Religion is, as such, fully dedicated to welfare of all.

According to circumstances pertaining to time and space, ways were established for salvation of man through many mediums from time to time. The establisher can be termed as Great man or Learned man. He may also be God-incarnate or messenger of God. This established a way for a religious community. All religious communities that we know today as Islam, Christian, Confucian, Parsi, Boddh, Jews, Sikh or Hindu etc. are religious communities and give separate directives regarding life-style in case a man aspires for all sided development. Although their ways may be different, their aim is the same.

Difference between religion and religious community is that religion originated with man, while community came into existence afterwards. Situation of religion remained uniform in the whole world whereas establishment of religious community took place from time to time according to the circumstances pertaining to the region and era.

A single force or element that can be adopted as per individual conviction was instrumental behind religion whereas there was more than one behind religious community. Religion is wholly dedicated to mutual cooperation, affection, unity, broad-mindedness, equality and welfare of all. Contrary to it, a religious community irrespective of being dedicated to all-sided development of man is bound by circumstances relating to the region and era and all the facts enumerated above, it has a limited span in comparison to religion. However, religious community happens to be an indivisible part of religion.

After knowing religion and religious community we can conclude that both are dedicated to welfare and all-sided development of man: it is another matter that there is a difference as to their comprehension. A religious community also does not cherish all-sided development pertaining to its followers without cooperation, equality, affection and unity into them. In this regard any division amongst followers of a religious community, whatever may be the basis and whatsoever may be the argument in favour of such a division, is in toto against the aim of the religious community.

The caste system, prevalent today in India, succeeds the ***Varna*** System and is based on inequality, non-cooperation, short sightedness and division. Exploitation is at its base. The basic spirit behind caste system remains to ensure maximum possible gain akin to selfishness for self and group of self that is -the people of one's own caste. It has accordingly caused harm to country and society for thousands of years. It has already divided us in about 3500 parts. It is quite amazing that attempts are made to relate it to religion or religious community. However, one, who has even a little intelligence, shall certainly negativate it on the ground that purpose and meaning of religion and religious community is to keep existence of man safeguarded and to achieve his objective.

Caste obstructs all this process. As such, religion or religious community-is quite non-related to caste system. Those, who try to affix seal of religion or religious community on caste system or wish to accord a footing to it, are ignorant of meaning and purpose of religion and religious community. Not only that, such persons, expressly or tacitly are not well wishers of society and nation. A perception of humanity happens to be incessantly far away from such persons.

Reference

1. This argument may convince those who believe in some divine power in respect of origin of man. Those who do not believe accordingly shall still have to admit that man could keep his existence in fact as per certain nice attributes in his nature. They may name these nice attributes as religion. Whenever man relented from accepting these nice attributes, miseries and disasters happened to be in store unto him. He could get pleasure and prosperity whenever he kept himself dedicated towards these virtues and he could resultantly enjoy development and progress.

2. Caste, Class and Problem of Establishment of Peace: With Special Reference to Indian Sub-continent

Needless to dwell in the remote past, but till today the division of human society on the basis of caste and class distinctions, has yet been subsisting as the main hurdle in the way of establishment of perpetual peace on earth. It is a worldwide problem. It is just possible that its form may be discerned differently in different parts of the world. It is also possible that the ultimate result or effect of this problem may appear to us somewhat distinctive in various regions.

In Western world as also in various Eastern nations, class distinctions perpetuate while mainly in Indian Sub-continent, human society stands divided on the basis of caste differences for centuries. The formation of castes has also resulted from class distinctions. In ancient India, that is, about four or four and a half thousand years ago, class distinctions could be seen in the form of ***Varnas***, which is not discerned today in its original form. In relation to the origin of ***Varnas***, the arguments, pertaining to role of divine power, have been given in various ***Vedic*** texts, mainly in ***Rig-Veda*** and ***Srimadbhagvad Gita***.

But as I have already dwelt at length in my article on ***Caste-System***, these arguments are in contradiction to each other. And eventually we arrive at the conclusion that ***Varna*** system was man made. No matter, there may be indicated numerous attributes therein, the division of the society on its basis, a feeling of inequality betwixt man and man was certain. Subsequently, this system was disintegrated. Today in the main nations of Indian Sub-continent – India, Pakistan, Bangladesh as also in Nepal, the successor of this system appears dividing the society into about four thousand parts and sub-parts. Along with inequalities there perpetuate serious social evils viz. exploitation and untouchability dwelling in the root of this system.

Certainly, human unity is disrupted as a result of its existence and perpetuation. In the beginning, that is, almost one million years ago, when human beings came into existence at a single place on earth, there was no difference of one person from the other. Neither, there was any class nor such a system, which may divide one from another. At that time all parts of earth were annexed with each other in one-way or the other. There prevailed an atmosphere of perfectly free human habitation. But soon, the anxiety for the safety of existence compelled human beings to unite and inhabit in a fixed place. Man began to dwell in groups. Collectively, the invasion, of any nature, was encountered. Certainly this led to the safety of existence. In human life the state of peace emerged. This was the most important change in human life. With this change, man passed a long period.

But, the above state of existence was not enough in human life. After the safety of existence, man had to advance on the path of development. Progress is the indispensable condition of human life. That is why; searching for adaptable atmosphere, man started to proceed in different directions, forming small groups. First of all the departure took place to the nearest places and then to distant ones. This was another important change in human life. Wherever man went, he added new chapters in history. Conclusively, whatever situation came into being is before us today. Today it may appear to us very much amazing because man has elevated the standard of progress in strikingly wonderful form. He has yet to advance on this path. To what extent the state will reach, probably, it cannot be estimated today.

The moment human beings migrated from one place in small groups, searching conducive environment for progress, the process of division was started in human society, although the visibility of state of division emerged after quite a long period. It is a common feature that a particular group of human beings, getting separated from the other ones, inhabited at a different place; subsequently, the direction of progress that they held, made the same segregated from other ones. Different places have different climatic conditions and the same affect the human body accordingly. That is why, with the passage of time, there appeared material differences in human groups, particularly relating to colour of skin, hair and physical length. Only one type of foodstuff, no matter be it the meat, is not available at a particular place, the same will have to be taken by the people, dwelling there. This also happened in the past and this led to the wide differences in the mode of eating. Not only this, due to the need of time or demand, the differences began to appear in human groups, owing to the established conditions and the systems subsisting in them.

All these differences, even after acknowledging divisions in human society, were the definite results of advancing and getting inclined towards the path of progress. I repeatedly emphasize this point of view. In this context, I negate in totality all arguments, which are given about the role of divine influence. This is beyond truth if any one says that he is born in a superior state by the grace of God.

By making a brief discussion on above topic, I only mean to say that none is born unequal from God's abode. All are born equal. By marching ahead on the path of progress, the state of differences originated which was likely certain. But this division cannot be compared with the division as we see today in the form of class and caste.

Now as first of all the process of division in society started from the moment of departure of human beings in small groups from one place to different ones, in the same way, it was the moment of induction of the word ***'own self',*** the process of emergence of classes came into being. The word ***'own self'*** can be used for a certain mobile or immobile property that is cattle wealth; plot of land or for any commodity etc. Whatever the arguments are given, intellect, physical power, interest, inclination, sincerity, competency and capability are the main factors for the development of a personality. And, all these attributes are not imbibed equally by every one. In establishing ***'own selfness'***, in the beginning, the above factors played a decisive role. Subsequently, ***'own selfness'*** was changed into ***'ownership'***. Plot of land, property and other commodities, even the men and women became the subject matter of ownership. Owner and subordinate became the two classes. The interests of both of them became contradictory to each other.

Now, if there is a question of accomplishing different interests in the classes, living in a single society, the state of clashes is bound to be brought about form time to time. And this actually happened. You may just imagine and view the history of Egypt about four thousand years before Christ, that is, the period prior to eight centuries from ***'Faraun Mainas'***. And not only Egypt, look at the regions, under the territorial limit of Mesopotamian Civilization i.e. ancient Babul, Assyria, Hittite, Phoenicia and Palestine, or Persia and India. After deep and intensive study, you may find my argument, more or less, to be true. In the texts and rituals of ***'Rig-Veda'***, the description of struggle between ***Tristsugana*** and ***Sthaniagana***, under the leadership of King Sudasa, is also a class struggle. But, peace is just the opposite condition of struggle because the basis of peace is mutual cooperation. That is why, in human society, for the people working for the establishment of peace, the class struggles have ever remained a great challenge. These are challenges for them even today, no matter the form and feature of classes might have been of any nature or in Indian Sub-continent, their place might not have been taken by castes.

We know very well that the classes, after creating divisions in society and repeatedly establishing traditions or customs, adversely hit the human values. Not only in economic and social sphere, but also in political sphere, making inequality as the basis, brought about the condition of an owner and a slave even between the offspring of one and the same Father, created the terrible state of exploitation and threw man miles away from the state of perpetual peace. In many Asian nations where there are followers of Buddhism, and evils like caste system and untouchability do not exist, there are class differences on the basis of economic status. Certainly this difference plays a decisive role in establishing the social status. In numerous Muslim nations and even in Western world, the situation is just the same. Contrary to this, in Indian sub-continent, caste, successor of ***Varna*** System creates all the more serious and alarming situation.

In Indian Sub-continent, four to four and a half thousand years ago, four ***Varnas,*** which assumed identical form with different classes, came into existence. Among them the first three i.e. ***Brahmins, Kshattriyas*** and ***Vaishyas*** originated from ***Aryans*** while the fourth ***Shudras***, were from ***Dravidians***. With the passing of time, amidst ***Aryans***, those who reached at the brink of economic backwardness or due to several other reasons, became socially inferior were enlisted in the category of ***Shudras***. Prior to the advent of these ***Varnas***, from North to South and from East to West, the inhabitants of Indian Sub-continent or ***Dravidians*** were not living under uniformity. By not living under uniformity, we should be clear in our minds that prior to division of Indian Society in four ***Varnas***, the people dwelling here were not within the sphere of a single class. They had no single or the same nature of religious or social system of living. Along with others, there were also the followers of Jain philosophy.

After the four ***Varnas*** came into existence, in Indian society, a new system was established which had rigorous and stiff rules far more than earlier. And within the embryo of that system, all the people of society were not enjoying equal status. Amidst four ***Varnas,*** the status of ***Brahmins*** was higher; **Kshattriyas** enjoyed second status and third and fourth ones were ***Vaishyas*** and ***Shudras*** respectively. ***Shudras*** were leading the most backward and sub-standard life. They were totally deprived of various economic, religious and social conveniences. It can also be said that they were under the clutches of different economic, religious and social restrictions. In other words, their social position was no less than slaves which later crossed all the limits of inhumanity'.[1]

And the above unfortunate state, of which direct and indirect bad impression was to befall in all the spheres of society for hundreds and thousands of years, the peace of the region was to be affected, which can be known and witnessed even today, was not gauged in all seriousness by the responsible people and their successors. The colossal and inestimable loss, which has been caused, which is yet in continuation, was ignored and is yet being done so. The scholars and intellectuals of the Indian Sub-continent, a land of the propounders of loftiest message of non-violence, consummated many wonderful researches and analyses, but they ignored the division of our society on the basis of castes and classes. The forlorn and decaying condition[2] of our society which is yet in existence; nothing was pondered or done for its amelioration by most of them. It is mainly true in reference to the scholars and intellectuals emerging from higher castes. Particularly, the role of social scientists has been quite deplorable. If not much, then the least should be witnessed by the social scientists, scholars and intellectuals, from the institutions like Parliament, Legislative Assemblies and other units[3], which are the basis of democracy. But they do not do so easily. It is because, knowingly or unknowingly, deeming the above state as real, they are keeping the same in their mentality. They are still not ready to change this mentality. But this state of affairs is not to continue forever.

In my article on Caste System, I have already dwelt on the subject that after the division of Indian Society into four ***Varnas,*** their rules were made quite rigorous. It was held to maintain the purity in blood through above rules. Besides food and customs, interclass marriages were banned which was not in accordance with natural laws. And as a result of such rules, not one but many such evils and bad habits originated which were against the principle of humanity too. Certainly these lead to obstructions in the way of establishment of peace. In this context, the state of Indian Sub-continent has been quite different from the rest of the world, whether you revert to middle age retrospectively or to contemporary period or to the present one.

Subsequent to the division of the society into ***Varnas***, whatever hard rules were framed pertaining to day-to-day practice, they were unnatural. They became the symbols of exploitation of mankind; evidently there was embodied the element of inequality in their root, being rigorous and unnatural these rules could not have lasted any longer. That is why, ***Varna*** System could not also exist in accordance to the spirit of framers. Before the period of Buddha, disintegration had started in it. The rules began to be disrupted. Castes emerged out of ***Varnas*** which later continued increasing. Sub-castes were also created out of the main Castes. Today the number of Castes and Sub-castes is about four thousand. That is to say, the society is divided into four thousand parts and sub-parts on the basis of inequality. Today, the roots of division are very deep. Not only this, whatever serious problems are there before the Society, there has mainly been Caste System prevalent at the root of majority of them directly or indirectly. The scholars, intellectuals and social scientists of Sub-continent will be able to comprehend its reality if they analyze the problem honestly. It is my firm conviction.

Let us view the existing state. Intellectual class is itself engulfed in the whirlpool of Casteism, which is very serious and unfortunate. Officials, people engaged in education world, even the Vice-Chancellors of Universities, are not free from the evil impact of Casteism. As I have already stated elsewhere, Parliament, State Assemblies and other bodies are within its grip. Hundreds of people who are considered criminals have entered the Parliament and Assemblies under the shelter of Casteism. Open struggles and numerous types of inhuman acts come before us endlessly on caste basis. Last time, about twenty-nine Caste-led struggles, occurred in Bihar, are before us wherein about two hundred fifty people were mercilessly massacred.

The young boys and girls who, by breaking the bonds of Casteism show the courage to marry themselves, many of them become subject to various sorts of victimizations. Recently in Mumbai a Sikh family mercilessly murdered a Sikh youth belonging to Scheduled Caste. Why? It is because that family did not like their so-called high Caste girl should marry a Scheduled Caste youth. Day to day such incidents take place, some of them come to the knowledge, most of them subside.

That is to say that for thousands of years Casteism has been the cause of different problems in society, which is yet in existence. Probably the extent to which this system has caused severe harm to the inhabitants of this Sub-continent, none else has done so much. If some one wants to achieve something on the basis of his/her strength, intelligence, aptitude, sobriety and competency, there is no reason of any objection to this. But everyone must find opportunity to acquire them equally. Without it, there is no possibility of establishment of peace. So I consider Castes and likewise existing Classes as the serious problem in the way of establishment of peace; I take them in the form of challenge for those working for the establishment of peace.

In one of my articles on Caste System lending my suggestions to get rid of it, I mainly said this that the so-called high Castes should change their mentality. Without bringing about attitudinal change, it is not possible to get rid of this curse. Whatever regular harm is caused in the spheres like social, political and cultural, due to Caste System, it is necessary to change our attitude to get ourselves liberated from it. But, as narrated, the change in the attitude will not possibly happen soon or so easily. What should then be done?

I have firm belief that education can play a vital role in this regard. Through education, gradually, the present and future generations will have to be acquainted with the reality of Caste System and the harms emerging out of it. So along with the people engaged in the work of imparting education, it is equally the responsibility of peace workers that they, taking Castes and Classes as a challenge, awaken the general people towards it, otherwise in their presence the problem of establishment of peace will remain existing.

References

1. In the 6th or 7th century before Christ. At this time, slaves were treated like domestic animals and their comparison was made with cows, horses, sheep and goats. They could be distributed in inheritance, could be sold to others, could be mortgaged, could be made targets in gambling and could also be given in charity. All sorts of inhuman atrocities were perpetrated upon them.
2. As a result of division.
3. After the ***Varnas***, Caste System came into existence, in which not once but several times the intellectuals were indiscriminately crushed. The benefit, which the region, the nation, the society or

human world was to gain from those of caliber, the above system, created hindrance in that. After freedom. India adopted democratic system of governance. For this, for the first time, in 1952, the elections for Parliament, Legislative Assemblies and for other units were held. From those first elections, the odious effect of Caste System can be clearly and properly seen in reference to above. After the election of ***Lok Sabha*** in 1952, and thereafter in a by election in 1953, Bhimrao Ambedkar's defeat was most shameful. It was the deplorable incident for the Indian Parliament, it deprived for people of the talent and caliber of a great intellectual. Not only this, several such illustrious figures, who could have beneficially proved a glory to nation by maintaining the dignity of Parliament and by working for the strengthening of democratic values, and for welfare of common men, could not enter the Parliament and Legislative Assemblies due to caste reasons. Jagjivan Ram was a competent person, not only in one but in so many fields. Let us just see the figures of his Sasaram constituency from 1952 to 1984. By and by the percentage of his victory went on decreasing. Why? You can well understand. In 1984 he could win election merely by 2 thousand votes. Subsequently he died. If he would have survived till the ensuing elections, I have no doubt but a belief that he might not have won from this constituency. The defeat of Karpuri Thakur in Samastipur, Bihar, the defeat of Charan Singh in 1971 from Muzaffarnagar [U.P.], the defeat of Ashoka Mehta from Surat constituency of Gujarat are the examples which express the evil effects of caste system. In 1991, a slogan was raised in Maharashtra, 'Maratha would be the Prime Minister', and so the Brahmins must be opposed. A wave flowed in whole of the province. Madhu Dandawate from Rajapur, Basant Sathe from Wardha and Vithal Gadgil from Poona were defeated. Parliament was deprived of the able personalities as these. The evil effect of caste system can be seen to the extent that Abul Kalam Azad contested election in 1952 from Rampur, a Muslim dominated constituency having 42% Muslim voters and among that majority was of the Sunny castes. He had to fight election from Faridabad [Gurgaon] constituency in 1957 having 25 per cent Sunni Muslim voters. Today the existing condition is before every one. What is the condition of Parliament in these days? It is not to be narrated. I can only say that in this process, the Caste System plays its dominant role.

4. Group of human beings going against the rules, framed by *Varna* System, went on becoming separated from it one by one. Along with the formation of their own new rules and systems, their separate Castes were formed. Castes were made not only amidst ***Brahmins, Kshattriyas,*** or ***Vaishyas***, but, amongst ***Shudra Varna*** too. Later, those not following the rules of their own Castes became the architects of Sub-Castes.

B

CULTURE AND CIVILIZATION

1. Indian Culture: A Perspective

'Culture' accords knowledge of basic sacraments of the human society or inhabitants of a nation. In other words, we can put this in this manner: through Culture, we gain knowledge of all those sacraments of human society or inhabitants of a nation, which guide their lives. If we peruse per point of view of words, we find that Culture-***Samskriti***- is derived from word ***'Samskara'*** and it denotes what I have already expressed.

Indian Culture is one of the oldest Cultures of the world; like cultures pertaining to Egypt, Mesopotamia, etc. It portrays its specific identity. Undoubtedly, there are those sacraments behind this identity that we find since their inception. What are those Sacraments? I hold that we shall inherently get knowledge relating to them in case we peruse Indian Culture chronologically in its historical perspective.

There are evidences from approximately four thousand B.C. regarding history of India and in context of lives of the people here. This era has also been described as ***'stone age'***. It has been stated in accordance with evidence that Indians had been living in form of tribes. It has also been accordingly stated that they used to carry out farming and cattle rearing. Above-mentioned evidences have been available after carrying out archaeological surveys at various places of today's Pakistan, Chennai, Gujarat, West Bengal, etc. Two things come out to be amply clear on this count and they are:

- *Indians used to live collectively; and*
- *They practiced non-violence.*

As we do not get very clear historical evidences of the above-mentioned era, we can put these two things in relation to Indians of that time -that is- Indians pertaining to 4000 B.C. had unto themselves sacraments of collectiveness and non violence.

Approximately, Indian History of 2500 years B.C. span is clearer to us and it portrays the mode or life-style here. This period is also famous as Indus Valley Civilization period. It has come to be known after archaeological exercises that both the attributes, mentioned earlier, were present in life-style even though in much developed form. Additionally, good management, planning and uniformity[1] are visible now. For example, city building has been systematic. There is a system that accords safeguard from natural calamities and other disasters. Animal-houses are there. There are cereal storehouses. Day-to-day acquired commodities are available in plenty. There is language, script[2] and religious philosophy[3] as well. There are also available significant evidences that classify that Indians had contact with persons inhabiting in other parts of the world and there was interaction among them.

As far as nomenclature for their inhabitants is concerned, the learned-people, subject-experts and historians differ. However, it is most apt to assume that these persons were ***Dravidians***. In addition to the sacraments of collectiveness and nonviolence in Indians in the era of Indus Valley Civilization [or earlier] we find other sacraments as follows and they clarify their culture. These are:

- Marching towards development;
- Good Management, planning and uniformity;
- Religiousness; and
- International Cooperation, which subsequently incorporated concept of ***'Vasudhaiva Kutumbakam'*** [This World is a family within itself permanently].

As believed, ***Aryans*** came to India in two thousand B.C. They came to India from Iran and naturally many sacraments came along with them. It can be termed in this way: they came here with a culture. ***Aryans*** definitely possessed expertise and cleverness. They had also capability of gaining knowledge uniquely.

They had contact with ***Dravidian*** Culture accordingly. ***Dravidian*** Culture and its sacraments were without ill effect irrespective of the struggles and acts of torture inflicted by ***Aryans*** and ***Dravidians*** on each other. ***Aryans*** adopted sacraments of ***Dravidians***, such as, non-violence, development-oriented attitude, good management, planning, uniformity, religiousness. It is also true that there the attributes of ***Aryans*** and of the sacraments that they came with, had great influence on ***Dravidian*** Culture of India at that time.

It was the impact of *Aryans* that usage of rituals, sainthood and faith began in the life of Indians. Era of knowledge[4] started. Comprehensiveness was the keynote in Worship-method, Philosophy was visualized and it mainly comprehended liberality. Above mentioned attributes of ***Dravidian*** Culture got intermingled with these attributes and ***Dravidian-Aryan*** Culture became Indian-Culture. Synthesis started from here onwards and subsequently it became foremost characteristic of Indian Culture.

In 4th Century B.C. Alexander attacked Northwestern part of India. He certainly conquered some of the parts. Resultantly, the Greek forces established cantonments in the conquered parts. This factor resulted in mutual impact between Culture of Greece and that of India. After that, the governmental Cooperation was instrumental towards bringing the two Cultures into union. Both Cultures had great impact on each other.

We can mention in this context Cultural attributes of Greeks, such as, bravery, philosophy, poetic-orientation, sculpture, theatre, architecture and authorship.[5] In the First Century B.C. after the demise of Emperor Ashoka the ***Shakas*** came to India from Iran. Subsequently, ***Kushanas*** came here. In the Fifth Century A.D. ***Hunas*** also came here from middle Asia. All of them established statehoods here in India and as ever; their cultures intermingled with Indian Culture. They became its permanent entities.

In Eighth Century, Arabs first of all came to Sindh. Sindh at that time was a part of India; now it is a part of Pakistan. The Arabs established their rule in Sindh.[6] Naturally; Arabian Culture influenced the people of Sindh. Arabs came here with Islamic Culture. As such, we can say that Islamic Culture came to Sindh and influenced its culture, that is, the Indian Culture. After that, constantly since 12th century, there has been an impact of Islamic culture on whole of India. Today, it is fully intermingled in Indian Culture. Brotherhood and internal equality happen to be supreme in Islamic Philosophy of life and so those are integral in architecture, dress and literature, which came with Islam. Undoubtedly, even today, many palaces, public places and private apartments are evident of mingling of both cultures.

It is also quite clear from it that Indian Culture is wholly integrator. It has been adopting good traits of other cultures, which came in its contact, while keeping its basic status intact. Not only this - as I have already mentioned -it has always been comprehensive.

Europeans began to arrive in India from Fifteenth-Sixteenth Centuries A. D. Portuguese, Dutch, French and English have been prominent among them. Subsequently, India was under the rule of Englishmen for a long time. Naturally some attributes of English Culture, such as, gentleness and time-adherences impacted our lives. Discipline and Internationalism, along with the development of education, have been there as a consequence of the influence of English Culture. Unity, transport, communication and political awareness etc. also developed and have become an integral part of Indian Culture.

In the same manner, Monghol culture also more or less influenced India. Not only Monghol, many other cultures, which from time to time came in contact with Indian culture, influenced it. Contact may be through many factors. We can mention in this context ideologies, beliefs and other mediums of contact besides mutual activities of commerce and visits.

When we state about impact of other cultures of world on Indian Culture for thousands of years, we must also remember that it was reciprocal. The Indian culture never abandoned its basic characteristics and as we perused, it patronized all adaptable aspects of other cultures and absorbed them completely.

The Buddhist philosophy and other religious thoughts have influenced not only Asia but more or less all regions of the world. These impacts were the consequences of social status or assumptions in India, which are fundamental base of culture.

We mention various developed and great cultures of World. It is possible that many may consider other cultures to be ahead of Indian Culture but the question remains - where do those cultures exist today? Many old cultures similar to Indian Culture are no more today. But, Indian Culture is alive even today. We mentioned Stone Age Culture in the beginning. We find Indians living a life of non-violence and collectiveness even then. This is to put in words thus: non- violence and the spirit of collective living were foremost in Indian Culture. These two are even today an integral part of this culture. We subsequently mention superior characteristics of this culture-these may include orientation to development, dogma of World-family, perceptions regarding liberality and knowledge-all these are even today integral part of that, it absorbed in certain salient features of the cultures in contact. This is a historical truth related to it.

Today, when we talk about the characteristics of Indian Culture, we get a definite picture:

- It indicates unity in diversities;
- It is integrator;
- It is comprehensive: away from shortsightedness;
- It is liberal and so it grasps pressures;
- It is all-welfaristic;
- It accords message of ***'Live and Let Live***' and propagates of non-violence;
- Truthfulness is supreme in it;
- This culture guides a man towards leading a peaceful and successful life. The guidance incorporates the operation of day-to-day activities of behaviour and conduct; and
- It leads man to peace that is the goal of life. The culture carries it by integrating '***knowledge'*** and ***'action'.***

As such, Indian Culture is unique and it is virtually a message for humanity as a whole. It bestows human life with above-mentioned characteristics, takes it towards pleasure and prosperity. After that, it directs life unto peace and eternal peace. On this accord, if we term it as ***'Wholesome'***, it will be a truth to an extent. In this manner, the world can learn quite a lot from Indian Culture and its call to assume whole world as a family can be definitely adopted by people all over the world. We must do so: it is in the interest of all.

As Indian Culture is dedicated to all, all belong to it; as such there is no danger to its permanence or existence. In my view, it is alive and shall continue to be so...

References

1. Marching towards south from north
2. It has not been readable up to now but it assumed to be ***Dravidian,*** which is different from today's ***Dravidian*** language-script.
3. There have also been available things, which establish usage of worship-houses, temples, and worship of Shiva, fire, water, trees etc.
4. ***Aryan***-treatises [***Vedas*** foremost] describe many aspects of human life, such as, origin, aim, goal, situation relating to the present life and thereafter and the life-style, worship, duties and exercises of conduct have also been discussed. ***Vedas*** are really store-house of knowledge and philosophy of the highest order.
5. Specially, authors on history.
6. It is another matter as to how the rule was established. Rule pertaining not only to Arabs or Mohammedans, but prior to that to Greeks, ***Kushanas*** or ***Hunas*** or subsequently to Monghols and Europeans. So many things have been mentioned in history about various attacks by above on India. But culture is a different thing. For it no one can be forced.

2. Indian Civilization at the Close of Twentieth Century

Indian Civilization is an ancient one, I am not the one to say so but world history testifies it. World history also tells us that Indian Civilization has had a unique identity of its own. While other civilizations have become extinct with time Indian Civilization has remained evergreen and continues to propagate the message of humanity. This prompted a poet to say:

"Greece, Egypt, Rome, All have vanished from this world, But still there are left, Signs of our existence"

Now, it is but natural therefore, that you ask, what are the signs identifying the unique identity of Indian Civilization? While still remaining evergreen, what message does it give to humanity? What are the reasons behind its survival? And, while we are at the close of Twentieth Century, what is its present condition? Before seeking answer to the above questions, it would not be out of way if we understand the meaning of civilization.

Meaning

Civilization is formed from the word ***'Civil'***. When the word ***'Civil'*** is associated with man, it certainly identifies certain qualities of him. Similarly civilization identifies those qualities of the inhabitants of a particular region or nation that are commonly found in them and additionally, becomes their identity.

Historical exploration has revealed that human beings inhabited India even during the prehistoric period. Even during the period that the historians have termed as ***'Stone-Age'***, there was civilization among Indians. A lot of information is available of the history of the past five thousand years that acquaints us with the Indian civilization during that period. During that period there were civilizations in the Nile Valley, Egypt, Valleys of Dajla and Euphrates, Babylon and Assyria or Mesopotamia and Greece too.

The history of the ancient Indian Civilization, about the period, of which we discussed above, tells us of many qualities of the inhabitants then. But the main among them was non-violence that accorded cooperation to the common man, and thus progressed.

Periodically, if we proceed further, we would find a blend of many other qualities in the inhabitants of India. In this blend the one that I consider being the main, is progressiveness. Indians have always prepared a conducive environment for this and will continue to do so in future too.

On the basis of the two above-mentioned qualities-non-violence and progressiveness, Indian Civilization became known to the human world in the ancient times and even today. Indian civilization harmonized with the qualities of various other civilizations. Not only ***Dravidians*** or ***Aryans,*** but Greeks, ***Shakas***, ***Hunas, Kushanas***, Monghols, Arabs and Europeans are with Indian Civilization, but it maintained its uniqueness.

History has witnessed many upheavals in India. Numerous examples of fundamentalism may be found here. India has experienced numerous External and Internal aggressions. But no one was able to destroy her Civilization.

Non-violence is an essential condition for not only existence but also for development and achievement of goals of human beings. It is permanently present in human society. It is the basic element of Indian Civilization. The collectivity found in the beginning of human society was possible only due to the fact that non-violence was the basic characteristic of the lives of Indians. Within its sphere, various streams of co-operation broke forth, transcending national boundaries, and a civilization that ensures existence, repeatedly stresses on collectiveness and urges co-operation at all levels, has a bright future.

We discussed about progressiveness too. This too has been a basic and important quality of the Civilization of India. The sphere of this progressiveness has been extensive, beautiful, unambiguous, harmonious and a symbol of unity in diversity; advancing continuously with the pace of development, the Indian Civilization remained harmonious and hospitable to everyone. It continuously sought concord so that the harmony of mankind might never diminish.

This is the reason that Indian Civilization kept attracting the human world towards itself, and as already mentioned in the beginning, kept it alive. Besides that it kept nourishing the qualities of other civilizations in India. In contrast, the civilizations became extinct at their respective places of birth and development. Numerous monuments, forts, arts and styles along with the different characteristics found among its inhabitants confirm the fact that Indian Civilization has nourished various qualities of different civilizations for a long period of time.

We are discussing the Indian Civilization in 20eth century. No doubt today its features do not appear to be the same as they were 2000 years ago. It is not surprising that it has not remained so, because as far as we can imagine, we will find continuous transformation. In other words, nothing is permanent. What appears to us to be stable for years, is actually not so. A living body becomes lifeless. It can be kept preserved with the help of chemicals but still, it is subject to continuous change. We would normally believe that a healthy person, in spite of his increasing efforts to preserve his body as it is, would never be able to do so. The body continuously transforms. The same principle is applicable to every other object in this world. I would like to repeat that nothing is permanent. Then, how can we expect the features of Indian Civilization to remain as they were?

But along with transformation, and even after the long march of progress, Indian Civilization is still alive for the reason that non-violence has been a permanent feature of it. And as already mentioned, it kept on exploring concord, kept increasing the harmony of mankind. Due to this reason, in spite of various invasions and upheavals, it not only remained stable, but also kept on reappearing more enriched than before. Even today at the close of 20eth century, it is appealing to the world, by displaying glimpses of its proud history, in which the harmony of mankind has been maintained and it has continuously created an atmosphere of concord.

II

Favourability, in fact, is the criterion that can preserve anything. I repeat that no living thing can ever continue to be in the same state. Change is compulsory. If there is no favourability, let alone progress even existence will not be affirmed. Therefore, as long as favourability is there, existence continues and progress goes on. As it starts diminishing, the pace of progress stops, downfall begins and finally the existence itself ceases. In the case of civilization too, this is absolutely correct.

As compared to other civilizations, the outstanding feature of Indian Civilization has been that it has always provided an environment conducive for non-violence and progressiveness. That is why it has lived on. If we look at its beginning[1] and its condition in subsequent periods, we would be able to realize the truth regarding the aforesaid statements.

What do we see about the ancient period[2] of Indian Civilization that we had mentioned before? We see that the Indians, after initially being flesh-eating hunters, slowly moving towards growing crops with the help of tools i.e., agriculture had become their foundation. Not only that, they also were involved in cattle rearing and engaged in building permanent dwelling. All this is possible in a conducive climate and environment i.e., on the banks of rivers, living collectively and co-operating with each other.

Now, let us have a glance on the period of Indus Valley[3] Civilization. You will notice that Indian Civilization has developed greatly as compared to earlier. Now not only of the villages, you will find development and extension of cities as well. From the point of view of concord, you would find systematic orderliness in the civilization, may it be in the field of construction, cleanliness, activities or bartering. Besides that, to ensure existence, there is sufficient emphasis on awareness towards non-violence, in this period. The presence of symbols representing '***God of Animals***,' confirms this fact.

Now, let us proceed to the ***Aryan*** age.[4] Here we have a new turn in progress. Striving towards cultural unity, for the sake of concord, we find that Indians were involved in literature, ceremonial rituals, arranging sequence of time and various other explorations. These explorations are associated not only with the earth but also with the Sun, Moon, Stars, Sky etc. and their effects on the inhabitants of earth. There is abundant knowledge regarding subjects like medicine, number system and also about soul, living-method, earth, heaven etc. among Indians.

If everything at all times remains perfect, how does one experience imperfection? The difference between perfection and imperfection should be realized. Not for one, but for many reasons and for the accomplishment of many purposes. In this context circumstances play an important role. Who are at the root of these circumstances? I am not going to delve into that argument. Yes, circumstances changed during and following the ***Aryan*** age[5]. The effects of imperfection multiply. It seems that selfishness and individualism were about to swallow the basic qualities of Indian Civilization. At that time Buddha and Mahavira did the task of reviving those basic qualities. Mahavira stresses on complete and genuine non-violence, where as Buddha infuses a different practical form of kindness into the hearts of the masses? Civilization again returns to its own path.

The Mauryan period[6] enters into a new age of progress through the path shown by Buddha and Mahavira. A new chapter in environment of concord begins. It was during this period that Greek Civilization came in contact with the Indian Civilization, and scholars like Panini[7] were born. Now theatre, sculpture, literature, plays and medicine, etc. present a beautiful yet realistic form of the civilization, according to the circumstances of the country and the transformed or rather refined ideology kept repeating the message of Indian Civilization.

Shaka, Kushana and ***Gupta*** periods[8], are those periods in Indian history which amazed the human world in terms of progress i.e. not only did literature find a new direction, but mathematics, Geography, Medicine and Chemistry made unprecedented progress. ***Ayurveda*** too developed quickly and many mysteries regarding Earth, Nature and the Skies were revealed. At this time many civilizations mingled with Indian Civilization and could assimilate its message of progressiveness and non-violence.

During the Medieval period[9] due to various internal and external difficulties, religious tendencies played an important role in keeping the basic qualities of the civilization in moderation. With the dominance of ***Vedic***-Hindu religious community, there was development of '***Jnana Marga***'[10] and progress of devotion; regional languages and mingling of Monghol, ***Huna***, Arab Civilizations and other with the Indian Civilization were the main events of this period.

Historians and other scholars review this period according to their point of view. They have every right to do so. But I sincerely believe that in spite of terrible conditions, Indian Civilization, along with its basic qualities, kept creating an environment of concord, as it was doing earlier. Personalities like Ramanuja were present who were not in favour of discrimination among the creation of God on the basis of caste or colour. They believed in equality, considered religious fundamentalism redundant even if it involved deep study of religious text and favoured simplicity.

During the period of Muslim rulers, the emergence of Sufism, which within the ambit of Islam, fully supported tolerance, and is an excellent example of the assimilation of the basis qualities of Indian Civilization. Besides that various Indian saints and scholars, who can be called the true representatives of civilization, created a favourable condition for Indians by harmonizing at various levels both in theory and in practice. We can include Kabir, Nanak, Namdev and Chaitanya in this link. All of them presented a perfect example of adopting the paramount principle of Humanity.

During Mughal period, royal poets and writers worked in order to strengthen the bond of unity, poet like Rahim is a unique example. Not only he but also poets like Faizi, Bedil and Gavvasi may be cited as examples in this context and we may call them as the true followers of the qualities of Indian Civilization.

Probably today's generation is unaware that Bedil totally condemned manslaughter in his works and gave priority to humanity. It is possible that at the governing level or by certain adherents of a particular religious community, there were fanatic activities, but the others who have harmonized with Indian Civilization have not been able to distance themselves from it and will not be able to do so in future too.

We all know that European civilization too met with Indian Civilization. Many of the effects of this convergence were beneficial. I will not discuss the political situation here, although I have been a student of political science. In the context of civilization, I would say that even during the period of British rule, it propagated the message of creating an atmosphere of concord. There have been attempts to tamper with Civilization. People, who themselves were nourished by it, tried to separate from it; selfish interest seemed to be gaining an upper hand and fundamentalism too became apparent but it also gave an excellent team, in the form of Gandhi and his associates, that lit the path of his country men on the basis of non-violence which itself has been a unique example of harmony till now.

India became independent. The world knows that it happened at a great cost[11]. India was divided into two parts. As a result many problems arose. Even then, India adopted a path of co-operation with the rest of the world in a novel way[12]. In the new age of internationalism, India became an equal partner and tried its best to strengthen international organization. This co-operation is the basic feature of its Civilization. Besides that in accordance with its Civilization India supported freedom, equality and welfare of citizens of countries all over the world. It opposed colonial and imperialistic hegemony and when necessary, raised its voice for its abolition.

We are, now, at the beginning of the 21st century. There will be many internal and external problems facing India. Not only India, most countries will have similar problems. In spite of unprecedented progress in various fields, the basic features of Civilization will probably face challenge. But it will certainly create conducive atmosphere for human beings as it has kept on doing from the very beginning. Indians will continuously be directed by its marvelous qualities, that is what I believe. Ups and down have been continuously witnessed and faced by this Civilization. At the close of the century too it is doing so. But it is flexible. Non-violence and progressiveness are its foundation. How will it not survive? It will and along with its basic foundations continues to encourage the world with the message of '***Live and Let Live***' and '***progress and allow others to progress***'. In other words, direct our path in new regulations and circumstances, by creating concord and accordance, just as it did from the very beginning. I have presented the historical matters briefly before you. I am confident that you would believe in what I have narrated, because my purpose of presenting the aforementioned matter was that you may understand that Indian Civilization continuously kept moving forward chronologically along with its basic qualities. Moreover, you might realize that in spite of upheavals, fundamentalism, aggressions and difficulties, it remained firm and continued to create human friendly environment.

References

1. About five thousand years ago.
2. *Ibid.*
3. Two thousand B. C. or earlier.
4. Following Indus Valley Civilization.
5. Known as the ***Vedic*** age.
6. Forth to second century B. C.
7. Author of the famous work entitled "***Ashtadhyayi***".
8. First to fifth century A. D.
9. Sixth to 12th century A. D.
10. This included acquiring of definite form by the six schools of Indian philosophy, arrival of '***Middle Path***' from Buddhist doctrines and development of scientific treatment and popularity of the theory of Shankaracharya.
11. In the year 1947.
12. According to domestic circumstances and changed global scenario.

3. Indian Culture and Social Life

Indian Culture is one of the ancient cultures of the world and due to certain unique features; it is still before us in its original form. Similarly, Indian social life has had an identity of its own and for centuries, it has taught many lessons to mankind. Many of these are not only important but worth adopting today. What are the unique features of Indian Culture? How it is still in its original form before us? And what are the lessons that Indian Social Life has taught to the human world, which are important, and worth adopting? Before discussing these questions, it would be better to know the meaning of culture.

Meaning of Culture:

Culture that is ***'Samskriti'*** as is evident, is derived from the word ***'Samskar'***. It describes the behaviour of the inhabitants of a human society or a particular nation. It is culture that identifies the behaviour of the inhabitants of a human society or a particular nation. For example: In relation to India it is often regarded that its inhabitants are never reluctant to accept a stranger as a guest and are hospitable towards him. Indians are followers of disciplined, decent and most importantly non-violent life style. They are believers of the principle of human equalitarianism. So, the above-mentioned features – honourable treatment to a guest, disciplined, decent and non-violent way of life and belief in the principle of human egalitarianism – are the basic characteristics or behaviors of people of India. When the rest of the world identifies these characteristics, it becomes ***'Samskriti'***, that is culture.

Basic Features of Indian Culture, Development in Various Faces and Impact on Social Life:

Regarding Indian Culture I have said that it is one of the most ancient cultures of the world. Among other ancient cultures there are Egyptian and Mesopotamian Cultures but they have now lost their original identity. Contrary to this, Indian Culture has still maintained its identity. And certainly, the reasons behind this identity are the basic qualities [behaviours] of the inhabitants of India, which can be seen since the beginning till the present day and which have influenced the social life here. What are these qualities or traits? We will get to know them better if we examine them in the context of the present, keeping in mind the history of the past.

Human history is traced back to ten million years[1]. In many Indian religious texts, there is mention of a period earlier than this. Moreover the period of human development[2] is fixed to be between 40 and 12 or 15 thousands years ago. These arguments remain between scholars and archeologists. In all these periods, India had human life, that too in its own way. But here I do not wish to confuse you with the ancient history that is not very clear, nor do I wish to confuse myself at this juncture.

It is not so clear but there are evidences of inhabitance or of social life of people in India that goes back to 5000 years B.C. or more. This was the ***Stone Age*** and on the basis of evidences, it is said that the inhabitants of India, at that time lived in tribes. They were engaged in agriculture and cattle rearing. These evidences are based on excavation and surveys conducted at various sites. Excavations conducted at several parts of [present] Pakistan, Gujarat, Tamilnadu [especially Chennai] and West Bengal print these evidences. Besides these, two things are clear too:

- Indians lived a collected life; and
- They loved non-violence

So, 5000 B.C., Indians had the qualities of collectiveness and non-violence. And these two, certainly, influenced the lives of people. On the basis of collectiveness, the people here faced difficulties collectively and also enjoyed pleasure together. And they were eager to progress on the basis of non-violence. Let me specify that agriculture and cattle rearing are the signs of love for non-violence and collectiveness in life.

We have with us more clarity, the history of 2500 B.C., which provides us the knowledge of the life style, which includes their culture and social system. This period is known as the Indus Valley Civilization. Cities revealed at Harappa and Mohan-Jo-Daro or Kot Digi[3], Kalibangan[4], Kathiawad and Saurashtra and excavations in south and east reveal that collectiveness and non-violence were present in the life style and social structure of Indians in a much-developed form. Besides, planning and uniformity[5] are also clear. We find that the cities were developed according to a plan. There were provisions to cope up with natural calamities, those too with collective means. Cattle shed and grain-houses were there. Items of daily use were in advanced state. Indians had language, script and religious philosophy. More over excavations reveal that Indians had contacts with inhabitants of other parts of the globe too. In this context we may mention the names of the cities of Mesopotamia, Turkmanian towns, Bahrain, Assyria etc.

Scholars around the globe are quite familiar with many features of Indian social life style, which include Joint Family System; custom of arranged marriages and religiousness. All these have been helpful in development or progress by collective efforts, facing challenges unitedly, nearness and feeling of unity, even though for different reasons. But now the joint families can be seen disintegrating, the custom of arranged marriages is weakening and the feeling of religiousness too seems to have been tainted. I, however, would like to mention here that 65% of India's population still lives in villages and a large part of village population still lives in joint families. In cities too there are joint families. In India the practice of arranged marriages is still prevalent that is the rate of divorce is comparatively low. Indian people are religious by nature. Why and what is being done by certain institutions to cause its decay is not the topic here, so I come back to the issue of culture and social life of the Indus Valley Civilization. As I have already mentioned, at this time collectiveness and non-violence were present in a larger degree than before. Besides, there were other qualities too, which explain the culture and social life of India:

- Constant strive towards development;
- Orderliness, Planning and Unity;
- Religiousness; and
- Contact and Business with inhabitants of other parts of the world, are the signs of the unique concept of Indian Culture and society – ***'the whole world is a family'***

With their advent[6] in India, the ***Aryans*** brought many qualities to this country. They had intelligence, skill and knowledge. ***Aryans*** themselves were proponents of unity and religiousness. Here the ***Aryan*** Culture with above mentioned features mingled with Indian inhabitants[7] and their culture and stratified the social life too.

Much is talked about many confrontations between ***Aryans*** and ***Dravidians,*** which I do not deny. But I can say with certainty that the intermingling of ***Aryan*** Culture with Indian Culture did not alter the fundamental or basic features of Indian Culture, i.e. the basic characteristics of Indian Culture remained unaltered. Collectiveness or non-violence, progressive outlook or other above-mentioned features, they all remained as they were. Moreover, they entered in ***Aryans'*** lives too. Besides, the way of life of ***Aryans*** was imbibed by the Indian culture.

From ***Aryan*** life style, tradition of rites, meditation, faith and rituals started in Indian lives. The stream of knowledge[8] burst forth. A new era began. There was much more comprehensiveness. There was introduction of philosophy in which forbearance and tolerance were supreme; the kind of introduction, which even today is important. In short we can say that ***Dravidian-Aryan*** Cultures became the Indian culture. From here began the cohesive outlook, which later became one of the main features of Indian Culture and social life.

During 326-25 B.C., Alexander fought battles on Indian land. He never realized his dream of victory although he did temporarily win some parts in Northwest. Greek camps were established in these regions. It was natural that contact was established between Indians and Greeks living in camps.

Even Alexander himself was impressed with many features of Indian life style. As a result Greek and Indian Cultures influenced each other especially in the war, philosophy, poetry, sculpture, architecture, theatre and literature etc.

In 232 B.C., Emperor Ashoka died. After him, ***Shakas***[9] from Iranian area arrived in India. After that came ***Kushanas***[10] and then, from Central Asia came the ***Hunas***[11]. All of these brought their own culture and mingled with Indian Culture. They gave their best features to Indian Culture and Social Life. Today not only Greek but ***Shaka, Kushana*** and ***Huna*** characteristics or features are also present in Indian Culture.

Arab too started to influence the people of India by establishing their rule and by living in many parts of Sindh and afterwards in rest of India. We may say that Arabs who brought Islamic Culture to India became a part of the cohesive Indian Culture, which now is a permanent part of it. In Islam fraternity or brotherhood and internal equality occupy supreme position. Additionally it has faith in one Supreme Authority. These features affected the Indians and became a part of its culture as I have already mentioned. Additionally the art, language, rites, sculpting, dress and literature etc. brought by the Muslims [Arabs] too affected the social life of Indians. The cohesive Indian Culture opened its doors to that culture also. Today many palaces, buildings and religious places are evidences in support of this fact. But I would say that in spite of being cohesive, the Indian Culture never lost its fundamental attributes or form, which it propagated before the world in the beginning. Whatever cultures came in contact with it, they adopted its good features, became comprehensive, and kept living though many of its contemporary cultures vanished.

Many Europeans brought their culture to India in 15th and 16th century. Dutch, English, French and Portuguese are the main among them. We know that up to 1947, India remained under English rule. It was obvious that European Culture especially English influenced the Indian social life. It happened. We can mention decency, punctuality and discipline in context of life style. Along with that, we can say that English Culture too strengthened the fields of education, development and globalization. Geographical unity, transport, communication and political awareness too prospered. Today, all this is present in the Indian Culture and social life permanently.

In India, especially the northeast, there was the influence of Monghol Culture. Not only that many others too influenced it from time to time, no matter what the basis of contact was. The basis may be trade or interchange of opinion or any other medium. But we should understand that when thousands of years ago other cultures mingled with Indian Culture, it influenced other cultures and the lives of people also. It never departed from its fundamental principles because these principles or features have been welfaristic for all. They have the capacity of patronage. That is why other cultures have been preserved in India.

Indian philosophy, system and sacraments have had influence on many parts of the world. We can see this influence by the intermingling of Indians – Greeks after the attack of Alexander. And why only then, before that too we find several examples in this regard. Then Buddhist philosophy and other religious thoughts influenced not only Asia but also all most all continents. These religious thoughts are the basis of Indian Culture.

In historical context we consider many great cultures of the world. May be they were more developed than Indian Culture. In this regard I can mention the name of Egyptian Culture whose some of the monuments are still incomparable. But the question is where these cultures are today? No where! They have vanished contrary to this; Indian Culture is alive in its original form and continues to influence the social life of Indians.

From historical chronological point of view, we started discussion about Indian Culture from ***Stone Age***. In that period we found non-violence and collectiveness in lives of Indians. At that time these great sacraments were principal or main subsequently, Indian Culture has remained constant for thousands of years. Subsequently, it has constantly been towards development, religiousness, forbearance and tolerance or the concept of global family-hood. Now, the picture of Indian Culture that emerges before us after the factual analysis of history is that it is:

- Symbolic of Unity in diversity;
- Cohesive or coordinating;
- Forbearing and Tolerant;
- All welfaristic; and
- Symbol of non-violence.

Additionally, searching for truth and ***'Live and Let Live'*** concepts are encouraged here. It has given directions to Indian social life and directed its inhabitants to treat on the path of religiousness so that they may be able to achieve ***'Peace'***, the aim of life, through continuous progress and by having their existence safe. It has been leading the way in day-to-day life and establishing harmony between ***'Jnana'*** [Knowledge] and ***'Karma'*** [deed].

Present Situation

Recently we have bid good-bye to the 20eth Century. Whenever some one departs or leaves, it is but natural to recall the events associated with the departed. The 20eth Century is unforgettable due to many events. Remembering it we will find much that is welfaristic but also much that is unfortunate. But at the close of 20eth Century, if we look at Indian culture, we find it giving the message of prosperity, happiness and eventual peace through its unique features, not only to Indians but also to the whole humanity. Indian Social Life is influenced by these features of Indian Culture and today the world that is suffering from so many problems, facing a number of difficulties can learn a lot from it, can accept its call to consider the whole world a family.

I agree that today the social life of Indians does not seem to lead by the features or characteristics and message of their unique culture; it seems that Indians themselves are becoming indifferent to it. It too seems that probably their behaviour is being directed from somewhere else. But I am confident that this culture that is dedicated to all will remain in existence, move forward and not only inspire the social life of Indians but step forward for the welfare of the entire human world.

References

1. Brief World History [H], Part I, p. 11.
2. Modern.
3. Now in Pakistan near Khairpur.
4. In Rajasthan Province.
5. Moving from North to South.
6. About 200 B.C.
7. ***Dravidians***.

8. ***Aryan*** philosophers and scholars not only presented many works to society but also meditated on topics like birth, aim or purpose of life; the supreme authority, relation to soul with Him, duties do's and don'ts etc. This knowledge is boundless and some of its aspects are everlasting.
9. First century B.C.
10. First Century.
11. Fifth Century A.D.

4. Impact of Indian Culture upon Thai Life

From the very ancient time, like Chinese Culture, all most all the main characteristics of Indian Culture have left their deep impact upon the lives of inhabitants of Thailand, earlier known as the Siam. The scholars, having knowledge of history of South and South-East Asia, are aware that the ***Khom Empire***, in which we can include today's Cambodia, Central Thailand, and many parts of Laos and Vietnam, was under the influence of ***Vedic*** values or ***Brahmanism***. When ***Vedic*** values were giving a new shape to Indian Culture calling Indians to adopt in their lives the virtues like theism, cleanliness, the process of development, comprehensiveness, to gain knowledge, to establish relations with others breaking the territorial limits of nations, and to give preference to forbearance and tolerance in day to day practices, they were also leaving their impact upon the lives of inhabitants of Thailand. This impact, later on became an integral part of Thai life. You can easily judge the same even today. In this context you need not to go far away. You can just see the practices of the royal family of Thailand. Every thing will become clear to you.

During the 3rd century B.C., Emperor Ashoka sent two Buddhist priests of high stature to propagate the ***Hinayana*** sect in Thailand, who reached Nakorn Pathorm, the then, capital of ***Daravadi*** Empire. And thus, Buddhist values, basis of which is ***Karuna*** [compassion], started their indelible impact upon Thai people. After acquiring a place in the culture of India forever, and after giving prosperity to it, Buddhist values overwhelmed the lives of Thai people. ***Panca Sila*** [***Panchsheela***] i.e., the five precepts, ***Tisikhha*** [***Triratana***] i.e., the three fold training, ***Kamma*** [***karma***] i.e., the law of action, four ***Garavasa-Dhamma*** i.e. four virtues for a good or ideal household life, four ***Brahma Vihar*** i.e., four principles for a great person or holy abiding, four ***Samgahavatthu*** i.e., four virtues for unity in the society, thirty eight -***Memkol*** i.e. thirty eight principles for prosperous life, side by side, ***Dasabidhrajadharma*** i.e., principles or virtues for a ruler, ***Cakkavatti-Vatta*** or ***Cakkavatti- Cariya*** i.e. principles [as duties] for an emperor, and above all ***Majjhimapatipada***, i.e., the Middle Way etc. can be mentioned here by me.

About 1000 Buddhist Era, ***Mahayana*** sect also reached to Srivichaya Empire of Southern Thailand which had its two headquarters- one at Chaiya and the other at Sumatra of today's Indonesia. For some time Lopphuri state also came under the influence of ***Mahayana*** Buddhism, however, later on whole region adopted the ***Hinayana***. Today, as we know, it is the State Religion of Thailand. Thus, thousands of years ago, along with ***Vedic*** and Buddhist values, Indian Culture entered Thailand. Later, it left such an impact upon inhabitants of Thailand, particularly in context of their day-to-day practices, that it became a permanent part of their daily routine.

As I have said in the beginning, along with Indian Culture, Chinese Culture also has left its impact upon the lives of Thai people and their day-to-day practices. But it never means that influenced by these two cultures, the inhabitants of Thailand lack in their own local Culture.

Thailand is one of the oldest countries of Asia. It has never been a colony. Its local values have their own significance. They have a prominent place among the Asian values. Like other Asian nations, ***'family'*** is the principal institution here also. It is expected here that each and every one in the family will discharge his/her duties, and will follow the characteristics of Thai life or cultural values such as ***bun khun*** i.e., an obligation of gratitude, ***chai yen*** i.e., cool heartedness, honesty, self-reliance and sincerity. All these characteristics are a part of Thai culture itself or of the Siam or of the ***Ayudhya***. Simultaneously, there is an impact of the great teachings of Chinese philosophers like Confucius, Man Tzu and Lao Tzu upon Thai people. And as said, right from the ***Vedic*** age, Indian Culture has been the basis of the lives of inhabitants of Thailand. Now it has been fully moulded according to the circumstances of this country. It has become its own, and it is sweetheart to its people.

5. Fundamentals of Civilization

Hundreds of thousands of years have passed since man has lived along with the creatures of different shape, size and kind. It is generally acknowledged that every being has a soul. What is a Soul? Where does it live in a body? What is its form? I leave these entire questions to you. You may decide to answer them according to your belief. But I can specifically say that even though the soul is embodied in everyone, the word civilized, the derivative of which is civilization, is used for man only not for any other creature.

In his preliminary age[1], which has also been acknowledged and described as natural or unrefined state, man like some other creatures lived on trees. He was bare bodied and had no permanent place to live. It is also a fact that he did not live on a particular tree and very often moved to another. In those days man was as fierce as any other wild animal, was carnivorous and ate flesh after having killed human beings. The raw meat, roots of fruit was usually his food. He moved about in a group as many animals did and they do so even now. In spite of it, man was different from other animals even then. The main reason of it was not only the formation of his body structure, but also the presence of the attributes of intellect and creativity in him. The intellect made him capable of analyzing things and the creativity made him dynamic. This is why man is very different from other animals. He learnt to make stone weapons at a very early stage and maintained them[2]. Besides he started collecting foodstuff also.

By making stone weapons man was able to achieve objectives according to his need at that time. They were useful for his self-security, and hunting to satisfy his hunger. In deed, the stone weapons proved useful to him to serve his purpose. In this chain of events, if we proceed further, we find that man later learnt to produce fire by rubbing two stones[3]. The fire thus produced served him in three ways: first to protect him from cold; secondly, to defend him to some extent from wild animals, though he was equipped with the stone weapons, but they were not sufficient enough to serve his purpose; and thirdly to enable him to cook his food particularly meat.

But having qualities of intellect and creativity and being different from other creatures, man was not civilized in his early years. There was nothing in him then to prove that he was superior in behavior or actions to other creatures. To be called civilized, it was necessary, even as it is now, to have good conduct in which morality is foremost. Therefore, Confucius[4] repeatedly emphasized that ***"a civilized person should refrain from those activities that are against the moral values"***[5]. It means that to be civilized one has not to forsake morality.

In the earlier period, during the course of his development, man could not make a significant departure from his way of life to be regarded as civilized and which could simultaneously lay the foundation of civilization. He was still making efforts '***to stay alive***' and '***maintain his existence.***' He did succeed a little as has been mentioned above. I would like to reiterate here that it was the intellect and the creativity that helped man to learn by his experiences and he started making further progress. Thus his path to become civilized opened out. In other words, we can infer that intellect and creativity played an important and decisive role in making a man civilized and in the evolution of civilization. I hope and believe that the scholar expressing their views on the above subject and the exponent of the philosophy behind it would completely or partially agree with the inference drawn above; it is another matter that the language and the way of their expression might be different. As an example, I quote here S. Radhakrishnan ad verbatim, ***"Civilization is a matter of mind."***[6]

II

Among all other beings man only has the quality of intellect and creativity. It implies that there is some power behind it, and that power is named God. There is no doubt that man represents the finest creation of God and He, besides granting him these qualities, endowed him with another excellent value also, the realization and application of which gradually brought improvement in his behaviour and development of moral values which eventually led him to become civilized. It also indicates the beginning of civilization. It is natural that you may ask what that value is or was. My only answer is that it was ***non-violence***, which is the fundamental basis of any civilization. So non-violence was the first and natural basis, while the second basis in the context of civilized and civilization was morality. It is also a fact that where there is non-violence, morality is naturally present.

As I have mentioned already, in his successive development, man discovered fire, which further ensured his safety. He was also able to protect himself from cold and to cook raw meat. In spite of this, he was not certain that it assured his safety. Man was still worried about his existence. He still wavered mentally and came out of this condition when an idea flashed in his mind as well as of his fellow beings that ***"they should live collectively to re-enforce their safety"*** and ***"living together, probably, became a necessity"***[7]. They gave the idea a practical shape. They started living together in a group and stayed longer at one place. It assured their safety. In steed of killing each other, they were now able to defend themselves collectively against any attack, particularly of wild animals.

Staying together collectively symbolized co-operation. Co-operation enhances trust. Wherever there is co-operation and trust, non-violence is certainly at the root of it. In the atmosphere of violence, there is no possibility of co-operation. Since non-violence is permanently in the nature of man, they thought of living collectively, let it be for the sake of his safety came to his mind. Contrary to it, if the non-violence had not been a permanent feature of his nature, idea of living collectively would not have come to his mind.[8] What would have been the consequences if, in spite of his attributes of intellect and creativity, he had applied his intellect negatively?

According to Gandhi, man himself would have been cause of his own ruin long ago[9]. But it did not happen so. Man grew in number because non-violence is permanently present in his nature. After having safeguarded his existence by living collectively, and having non-violence in his nature, man applied his intellect and creativity freely for his further development. On his way to become more civilized, he fortified himself with other excellences of character by setting up various systems, not forgetting to maintain morality. On his long journey to progress, man discovered an environment conducive to him and made efforts to achieve his goal. Whatever he has achieved so far is before us.

We should not forget that at the elementary stage man learnt to live with other human beings collectively and to stay at one place longer than before, he co-operated to his safety or his efforts to achieve his goal. Co-operation does not mean depending on others, but working together freely. Hence, the third fundamental basis of the rise of a civilization after non-violence and morality has been '***equal freedom to all.***' John Locke, the philosopher of 17th century had different views about freedom. According to him, ***Freedom means that I should be able to act according to my own free will in all spheres of life so long the law does not prohibit it, and that I should not remain subjected to anyone's fickle uncertain, unknown despotic wishes***.' His statement appears to be incomplete unless the above-mentioned wish of a person foresees the same for others. Since time immemorial, the meaning of freedom, in fact, has been that a man himself should be free and make sure that others also are free like him.

Therefore, Non-violence, Morality and Freedom are the three fundamental basis of civilization. By depriving others of their freedom by violent means subduing them by immoral ways, no civilization can be created nor can it be nurtured. We have before us the history of thousands of years that tells us that whatever efforts have been made to subject others becoming indifferent to non-violence, which is the basis of peace, the civilizations had their downfall. As opposed to it, whenever man has faith in the fundamental basis/principles. As a case study, let us discuss in brief the rise and fall of Egyptian and some centers of Mesopotamian Civilizations.

III

Rise and Fall of Egyptian Civilization

Rich in minerals and advanced in agriculture, the Egyptian Civilization, like Indian and Mesopotamian ones, was the most developed civilization of the world. About four thousand years B.C., several communities called ***'Noams'*** came to be known for the progress they had made through co-operation with one another. From these communities there emerged two states in the north and the south for leadership, which the southern state overcame the northern one and Menus set up a powerful kingdom in Egypt. As I mentioned before, Egypt was an agricultural country. After Menus had set up the kingdom, many plans for systematic cultivation of land were made. From the point of proper administration, farmers were divided into several groups. The administration of each group was in the hands of a high council. The council acted as a go-between especially in connection with the collection of taxes from frames and payments to the government.

In other fields also administration was carried out in a systematic and planned way. The advisory board was constituted inclusive of other Chief Advisor, Chief Treasury Officer, the Chief Justice and other higher Officer to advice the King. It was due to the good administration and implementation of necessary conditions for an overall development and progress of Civilization that Egypt made an astounding progress. Its Civilization became sky high. It was the time when the wonder of then world, the pyramids were built. Even today seventy pyramids have remained among which ***Khufu*** pyramid is the biggest. It is 146.5 meters high and 2300000 stones were used to build it. It took twenty years to complete it.

The Egyptian Civilization was sky high during this period and it was not possible for it to rise further or maintain its current position. The people of Egypt became indifferent to the basics of Civilization. ***Noam*** communities started fighting with each other and tried to undermine each other's position. The result was that the government at the centre became unstable and became weaker and weaker. The unity of the country was shattered and the Civilization met with its downfall.

About two thousand years B.C., Egypt was again united, but this time unit was not the same as was achieved by Menus. Naturally, in spite of the extensive system of irrigation, craft and expansion of commerce, the process of development could not be maintained for long. There was resentment among masses because of the partiality shown to certain communities by the administration. People by large were dissatisfied and were unable to develop their Civilization as before. Like the unique progress made in the fields or writing, architecture, arithmetic, science, astronomy, and medicine after the unification of country by Menus could not be regained[10] and because of dissatisfaction of masses and their resentment, the mutual co-operation continued waning and the distance among them growing. Taking advantage of the conditions, an Asian tribe[11] invaded Egypt and subjugated it.

Having remained subjugated for a little less than two centuries, Egypt gained independence under the leadership of Ahamose-First. After it, during the reigns of Ahamose-First and Tuthmomis-Third[12] it had also become a military might. The then rulers mussed it in conquering the adjoining areas and some parts of Asia, plundering them and exploiting them by making people slaves. The great achievement of the then Egyptian Military might was the organization of Navy and the induction of a variety of ships in it.

The Egyptian rulers who were indulged in attacking and plundering could not stabilize the internal administration. They could not share freedom with the people at large. Under these conditions, Egypt could not make any progress further and lagged much behind the earlier successes. The inner conflicts weakened the nation and about one thousand two hundred years B.C., it was exposed to foreign invasions and subjugation and the Egyptian Civilization met with its downfall.

IV

The world famous Mesopotamian Civilization prospered in the Valleys of the rivers Tigris and Euphrates [***Dazala and Farat***]. In the south of it, the Sumerian Tribes developed a unique irrigation system, perhaps for the first time, by constructing reservoirs, dams and canals and gave new dimensions to farming. They had a well-developed system of cattle rearing and had methodically separated the cattle required for agriculture. They had a system of taxation and a very civilized way of living. About four thousand B.C. there were twenty or twenty-five small kingdoms, which were ruled by priests. They were called ***Patessi***. It was during their reign that their Civilization was reckoned as one of the ancient Civilization of the world. Later on, the two powerful kingdoms, the ***Lagash*** and ***Umma***, had a conflict just for the reason that both wanted to bring the whole of the Southern Mesopotamian under their rule. This sort of thinking was against the fundamental basis or the principle of civilization. The above kingdoms fought with each other for a long time. In such an environment full of strife, further advancement was not possible. Along with that, in an atmosphere of violence, there was always a possibility of damage to whatever progress they had already made. And it happened there. Also it affected the areas of the Southern Mesopotamia. One of the ancient and renewed civilizations lagged behind. It was about 2500 B.C. Sargaon-First, Who was the ruler of ***Akkadi*** tribes, inhabiting the Central and North-Western Mesopotamia, vanquished the Sumerians and ruled over them.

During the reign of Hamurabi, which was between 1792 and 1750 B.C., Mesopotamia was integrated once again. He was a great and an autocratic ruler who conquered the smaller kingdom of Mesopotamia and brought them under one banner. Though he united them by violent means, he ruled over them according to law. His Code of Conduct containing 282 laws gives an insight to the social, political and economic organization of the then Babylon. The city of Babylon became famous all over the world as the center of casual, political, economic and cultural set-up. During his time, religion, literature, culture and science all progressed excellently. Not only this, there was development in other fields also and the civilization that had earlier lost its brilliance flourished once again. He achieved this goal by paying attention to the development of other areas also like architecture, crafts, trade and commerce besides agriculture. Many literary works of that period are still found. The most famous among them is '***Gilgamesh***' which depicts the story of deluge [***Mahaparalaya***]. Besides these achievements, mathematics, astronomy and others too were at their peak. The ruins of Babylon tell the story of its once prosperous Civilization. During the reign of Hamurabi, the Babylon society achieved the highest goal of its development and it is regarded as the golden period of its history. It is an anomaly that it did not last long. Babylon had to face many invasions, which caused the downfall of this great civilization.

In 18th century B.C. the Assyrian kingdom emerged around Ashar, a city in Northern Mesopotamia. During the reign of Tiglath Pilessar-Third [745-729 B.C.], who had conquered Babylon, this kingdom started making progress and it continued further during the reigns of the later kings chiefly, of Sargon-Second [722-705 B.C] and Asaruhddin [680-669 B.C.]. Roads were systematically constructed, canals were dug, many cities developed and there was international expansion of trade. Consequently, it once again attained its glory and became a powerful and prosperous centre of the world. But it is unfortunate that later on because of mismanagement and mal-administration there was exploitation of the general public and this kingdom also disintegrated and the great civilization perished.

The development of a civilization is not due to the efforts of an individual, but is the result of the collective efforts of more or less every member of society. As everyone in one-way or the other contributes to its development, the credit of it should naturally be given to all. Everybody wants his personal freedom and his peace should not be disturbed as one of the permanent partners of civilization. But when someone chooses the course of his progress for his own peace, development and prosperity by exploiting others, in that case the civilization however great and prosperous it might be faces problems and subsequently such civilization declines.

I have quoted above a few examples from the Mesopotamian Civilization. The purpose of it is that we should have a clear understanding of those factors, which are essential for nurturing a civilization. In fact, they are the ones, which I have discussed above in the beginning, and they are the fundamental principles. Non-violence is the foremost among them; the others are morality and freedom, which are related to it. All great civilizations of the world whether of Greece, Egypt, China or India, they prospered on the basis of these principles and any action antithetical of these principles causes their down-fall from time to time. People deviated from the path of non-violence, became immoral and deprived others of any civilization however prosperous it might be if it is indifferent to non-violence, morality and freedom to all. If we want to be recognized as civilized or are proud of our civilization, it is necessary that we must be mentally inclined to non-violence as our ancestors were. Even today, to have moral values and to ascertain freedom for others is as essential as it was for the human beings earlier.

V

There are many chapters in history that describe the end of many civilizations caused by indiscriminate foreign invasion. I would not like to mention any particular state or nation; but would like to emphasize that by these barbaric invasions where violence played havoc, the immorality crossed the limits and the freedom of human beings was totally ignored, no invader has been able to annihilate any civilization. India at least is the living example of it. India has faced a number of barbaric invasions, but none of them could destroy the Civilization of this country, which is unique in its unity in diversity. Of course, these invasions proved detrimental to its Civilization, from time to time, but the people passed the test successfully and made it up in a short time. The fact is that a civilization has its downfall when its own fosterers do not follow the fundamental principles of civilization. It is an ultimate truth.

References

1. About one million years ago.
2. These weapons made of stone were primitive, crude and unshielded. Therefore, we can say that these stone weapons were sharpened pieces of stones weighing two or two and a half kilograms.
3. In Paleolithic period.
4. Kung-Tse or Kung-Futsi [551-479 B.C.] was a famous ancient Chinese philosopher who propounded the '***Doctrine of Moral Politics***' making ***ZEN*** [humanity] the basis of mutual relationship among men and gave supreme place to morality.
5. A History of Political Doctrines [H], Part-1, p. 132.
6. S. Radhakrishnan: Speeches and Writings [May 1962-May 1964], Publication Division, New Delhi, 1965, p.430.
7. It is quite different from the views of J. J. Rousseau, the French Philosopher. He writes that in primitive stage, co-operation with one another was not a necessity for people and that whatever one needed was a part of ones instincts. [History of Political Doctrines [H], Part-2, p.191]
8. Thomas Hobbes mentioned in "***Leviathan***" that ***'man has a natural tendency to call for the maintenance of peace for his safety.'*** Therefore, man first thought of living collectively and put a check on his struggle.
9. Young India, 2 January 1930.
10. The Civilization of Egypt under the leadership of Menus once again attained unprecedented heights and was regarded as the best civilization of the world. Besides building pyramids script was invented. The Egyptians made use of certain signs and pictographs

in writing. They developed a single script and made progress in fine arts. Magnificent temples as in *KANARK* were built. They were adept in *decimal* calculation and were familiar with the fundamentals of science. They calculated areas of triangle, parallelogram and circle. Calculating the movement of planets in the sphere, they prepared an ephemeris in which a year was divided into twelve months and three hundred sixty five days. They had also made great progress in the knowledge of human physiology and surgery.

11. Known as ***HIKKOS.***
12. The period of reign was between 1525 and 1491 B.C.

6. Cultural and Economic Relations between India and China

India and China are two big countries not only of Asia but also of the world. They are two neighbouring counties and both have also preserved their five thousand years old Cultures. They are agricultural countries and a great majority of population is rural. The lacs of villages spread all over the country and the rural population have been the main resources of the cultural expansion as well as of the economic growth of their respective countries.

The authentic details of India's cultural evolution are found in Indus Valley Civilization [2500-2000 B.C.]. Then comes the ***Vedic*** period [2000-1500 B. C.] when we get the glimpses of intermittent details of the cultural development. The first detailed and historical phase of China's Cultural evolution was Shang Yin era [1765-1122 B.C.] and during the period of Chou [1122-756 B. C.] Chin [246-210 B.C.] and Han [206-220 A.D.] the Chinese Culture touched some great heights of attainments. This period of Chinese Cultural evolution saw the development of the great philosophies of Confucius and Tao and marks the beginning of coordination between these philosophies and the Buddhist values. This kind of coordination found a parallel in India where the two great cultures ***Dravid-Aryan*** coordinated well with each other about 2000 B.C. and later the other cultures that reached India from time to time harmonized with Indian Culture so well that they became one with it.

The characteristic of harmony that Indian and Chinese Cultures achieved thousand of years ago made a great impact on the other countries of the world. As China and India are neighbouring nations, the quality of harmonization had a particular influence on the masses of the two countries. It can be noticed in the lives of the people living in the Northwestern regions of India and of those living in the border areas of China.

The Indo-Chinese relationship was established long ago in the ancient times, on the basis of the quality of harmony present in both the cultures. It will require writing a big book to tell in detail about the long-standing cultural ties. However, I would like to mention in brief that it was in consequence of the profoundness of these cultural ties that hundred of Chinese scholars were the student of the famous Nalanda University much before the advent of Christ. The Chinese scholars participated in Buddhist Congregations [***Sangeetis***] ahead of others. They were the centre of attraction in the forth congregation [***Sangeeti***] held in Kashmir during the reign of Emperor Kanishka in the first century A.D.

From the time onwards and up to the 19th century, the scholars of the two counties visited each other and strengthened the cultural relationship. In ancient times, if the Indian scholars like Dharmaratha, Kumarajiva, Buddhajiva, Dharmakshema and Sanghabhuti visited China, the Chinese scholars Fah-Yan, Sung-Yun, It-Sing and Huentsang came to India. Among them Huentsang was the

Chairman of a Buddhist conference sponsored by the Indian Emperor Harshavardhana. It is not all. The way Huentsang and Fah-Yan enriched the Indian history by their writings, they became an inseparable part of it. In other words, the Indian history is incomplete without a mention of them. I am, therefore, in a position to say that the Indo-Chinese cultural relationship is not a past event of history but a reality even now.

II

India and China are prosperous countries in many areas and the economic ties between them were established long ago along with their cultural relationship which afterwards became firm. In this regard, the first evidence can be traced to ***Magadh-Maurya*** era [5th and 6th centuries B.C.] in India. The ***Gupta*** period [5th century A.D.] shows further improvement. We all know about the economic and trade relationship that existed between the two countries since then to the first half of the 20^{eth} century. It will not be of much relevance to discuss them here in detail.

After the Second World War the economic order of the world underwent a great change. Especially in the new economic situation India and China emerged as two great powers. It was a period of transition and it was extremely necessary to open a new chapter, but unfortunately there developed an atmosphere of bitterness. Why? It is not relevant to discuss the reason here, but I would like to add that in spite of this bitterness the two countries should not ignore the long and firmly established ties between them, nor can they afford to do so.

The Sino-Indian economic relationship improved again towards the ninth decade of the last century. The Indian

Prime Minister Rajiv Gandhi in 1988, the President K. R. Narayanan in May 2000, and the Prime Minister Atal Behari Vajpayee went to China on official visit in June 2003, and Mr. Li Peng and the Chinese Prime Minister Zhu Rong came to India in June 2001 and January 2002 respectively. These visits gave new dimensions to the improvement of relationship between the two countries and the trade relationship is improving day by day. The exchange of trade which amounted to 3 billion dollars per annum five years ago has now gone up to 10 billion dollars per annum. This is good indication but it should be raised further. There is every possibility for it; especially in the development of infrastructure for the increase of trade between the Northeastern regions of India and Western China. The under developed regions of Burma can also be included in it. In this direction, the topic of opening of Nathula trade-root has come up. It is a very important issue that would prove an early solution and beneficial also. It is the demand of time that the two governments should sit together and think of some more measures, as this and the participation of non-government agencies should also be encouraged.

III

Chinese economy is considered to be an advanced one in the world. It has maintained the growth rate of 7-8 per cent for the last 7 years. India's economy is also fast-moving. It has also the growth rate of 7-8 per cent per annum. But there is still a big challenge for both the countries to bring the rural population economically at par with the others. Both the countries can cooperate with each other to a solution of this problem.

The Sino-Indian economic co-operation is now indispensable and their cultural ties can be the basis of a firm foundation for it. The liberal Chinese Government at present is well aware of the importance and cooperation of India. Therefore, the steps they have taken to have good relations with India on the basis of mutual accommodation are praiseworthy. India also recognizes the importance of China in the economic order of the world. They also have a keen desire to solve all problems by mutual discussion and create an environment for long lasting cooperation between the two countries.

The untoward happenings in 1962 created an atmosphere of mistrust in India for their neighbouring country, which more or less still persists. It is essential to transform this mistrust to trust. If it is achieved, relations between the two countries would strengthen and would prove to be beneficial to both of them.

C

PHILOSOPHY AND RELIGION

1. Gautama Buddha: Human Religion and Peace

A consideration has been continuing since utmost early stage of human life. The consideration is regarding controlling others. A person wants to keep him or herself in a higher position in comparison to others. This factor has been responsible for disintegration of society. Many nations faced degradation on this accord. A person forgets that he cannot be master of others. He is master of self-only. Sooner or later, we shall have to admit and adopt the concept of equality and it indicates friendliness. Lord Gautama Buddha preached this in times past:

> ***"Attahi Attano Natho Ko Dwinatho Parosiya; Attana Va Sudanten Natham Labhati Dhullabham"***

That is: ***"Man is himself his master. No other one can be his master. Hard earned mastership is gained only after sublimating oneself adequately"***.

Lord Buddha was in favour of equality amongst all human beings. **'*Man*'** or **'*woman*'**, all were equal for him. There was no caste or class in his vocabulary. He was not only deadly against the words - master and slave; he struggled during whole of his life to eliminate them. It was during this struggle that he established human religion based on equality in order to ensure that all may tread path of peace. He wished that no one should exploit any other. All must control themselves. We must give up desire to become masters: such a desire is false and should be given up heartily.

There has been a tendency in human society to control others or to keep others as slaves. This tendency has been there since quite long. The tendency has been at all levels: personal, social and national. It was on this account that not only human blood was shed in personal, social or national struggles but societies were also disintegrated. The existence of humanity was challenged and its peace was disturbed.

Lord Gautama Buddha induced human beings to know his reality. He did not permit concealment of innumerable evils that emerge from policy of non-equality. He stressed perpetual need of equality based on affection and friendliness. He propounded this as Human Religion. It is a remedy to all problems. He initiated a non-violent movement-cum-revolution against mastership spirit of human beings. A particular class had been keeping its all-out hold on society. This class had been prescribing false and selfish rules again and again. Human society was being made fearful of God in order to achieve selfish goals. Lord Buddha alerted this class and stated:

"These persons believe in one God. We can be up to that God only through them. The Human Beings can enter 'Pawana Pawananam' only after their permission."

It was, as such, made mandatory for people to offer them things in form of ***dakshina***. They were required to worship them and to be on the way shown by them. They were as a way asked to give all of theirs to them.

"This tendency of such persons in World-history is like that of a beastly thirsty and hungry lion. This is actually the nature of people who consider themselves born to exploit others. These persons prescribe and manage thousands of regulations."

He said:

"They are motivated to establish their hold on society. They want control on the people in any deliberate manner. They describe simple regulations in a complex way so as to keep their position intact. They produce stories before people for this very purpose. The stories are framed in a way so as to get their doctrines confirmed. Thereafter, they combine these stories with human service pertaining to others so that people may remain obedient out of fear. How sweet the dream shown by them is - they say - in case a person wants to flourish in his life and wishes to be in heaven after death, he can expect so only through them. The people shall have to perform various rituals and rites etc. in accordance with the path shown by them. They have made life so unreal and complex. They have made mind so perplexed that life cannot go on adequately - this can be straightforwardly stated. A man can learn nothing except dissatisfaction. This is like reducing a man in a state of idiotness after intoxicating him very gravely."

Gautama Buddha came forward to save human society from these rites and false rituals etc. He said.... A man shall get welfare in proportion to his being away from these vices... Lord Buddha accorded such a warning against the class that was arbitrary. Distressed people at large at once comprehended that. They put their attention to what he said. Lord Buddha continued struggle against the class dominating since centuries in a broad perspective - this class was exploiting human society arbitrarily. He achieved victory ultimately. Human religion based on equality could spread itself and the concept of peace could find its way.

That class in Buddhist era was in favour of policy of inequality in humanity through false rituals or regulations etc. The people belonging to this class were not in favour of equality to all. A spirit of fear was forced unto people's mind through attractive things like God, or Heaven. The so-called higher class did these things. A particular class was not permitted to exercise rites, activities pertaining to education or to perform rituals. Behaviour towards them was worse than that towards animals. The people belonging to this class were called ***Shudras***.

All know that it was prescribed.... no ***Shudra*** should get even a word of ***Vedas*** in to his ears. If so happens in any eventuality molten lead must be poured into his ears. This class could not reside with other classes. The persons belonging to this class were refused to eat with, keep company or sit with persons of other classes. This class was without rights. The position of this class in society was next to animals. Lives belonging to this class were dedicated to one aim: this aim was to remain subordinate to the will of other classes and to do whatever people of other classes would want. A person belonging to ***Shudra*** class could only breathe as per their indications.

Ultimately, Gautama Buddha could not tolerate this all. He perused ghastly sin in this policy of inequality. He had acquired intellect and energy. His heart was as open as the open sky. He observed the extent of unjustness in those who were leading the people. He could also realize a feeling of glory in them along with their unjust power. Afterwards, Lord Buddha opened his mouth fiercely and cleared the way to human society through compassion and affection. Gautama did not want to force any right on anyone.

He intended to break spiritual and mental obstructions pertaining to humanity. It was for this reason that open hearted Buddha suggested ways and means to salvation and liberty to those persons who were downtrodden and devoid of rights. He suggested simple ways and means through his exquisite intellect.

Lord Buddha could know the real reasons that aggrieve us. He searched a way to put an end to agonies. He collected the treasure of all solutions in his great mind and thereafter opened that way equally for all without any distinction. He was a master. He inspired all to gain "***Sambodhi***" peace. Such a person, Lord Buddha, was - an inspirator who was peaceful, one who sermoned human religion and who could accord liberation. He said:

> ***"Jachcha Na Baslo Hoti, Jachcha Na Hoti Brahmno; Kammana Baslo Hoti, Kammana Hoti Brahmno"***

It means - **"No one is *Brahmin* by birth. No one is low. A man is *Brahmin* or low as per his deeds"**.

Mahatma Buddha, who accepted the doctrine of "***Karma Shreshtha***", achieved a victory by stipulating human beings as equal in struggle between priests or saints and then Lord Buddha paved an easy way that was for emancipation of humanity. It has been described in Lord Christ's '***Sermons on the Mount***' as well as in the ***Gita.*** The priestly or saintly class had negated it. This class had adopted the diction pertaining to ***"great by birth and position by fate"***. They had expressed that no truth could be known by simple or straightforward way. These people used to talk about 2000 hells and heavens and public in general was dreadful of them. These people used to suggest that salvation of public was possible only through the ways prescribed by them. Only then they will get entry in to heaven or shall have to suffer hell.

Innumerable persons of society were in want of knowledge vividly. The sphere of ***Vedas*** had been made limited and mysterious. The human society was chained to misbelieves and deceptions. Lord Buddha gave the message to human society of leading life through non-violence, compassion, affection and intellectual ingredients. Non-violence, compassion and affection are true and fundamental assumptions. These assumptions are sacred and non-complex. They are mighty basis of human religion. Lord Buddha adopted these basic assumptions in his sermons. People grasped his sermons in general very soon.

Behaviour of Lord Buddha was simple but that of equality. His language was that of a common man. His tongue became sacred on this account for all: educated and non-educated or rich and poor. Undoubtedly, Lord Buddha raised the voice of perpetual compassion and peace on this earth, which was suffering and was under duress. He visualized agony and its cause. He clarified sacrifice and saintliness of high order. He gave truthfulness of indifferent order, welfare of others and sublimity to human character.

These were means to liberation. He made people understand the factors behind disasters and cause of agonies. He stated that whenever there is some grief or disaster, we must clearly understand that there is certainly some evil within ourselves. As such, we must know both "***Samvrattik***" and "***Pramarthik***" truths.

Lord Gautama Buddha advised people to ponder over their shortcomings and said:

"We very easily see a defect in others. It is difficult to see any shortcomings unto self".

A man spreads shortcomings of his neighbours like straw whereas he tends to hide any shortcomings unto self. The truthfulness of life lies in the fact that a man should examine his own shortcomings and causes of agony.

Lord Buddha dedicated himself to eradicate many evils including that of finding faults with others. He also conveyed a message about absolute integrity through non-struggle device. He stressed upon understanding the reality of this life without any discrimination. His message was for all. Human equality was not only a message of his religion: it was also an all-sided basis.

Morality is integrally connected with humanity. In case it is separated from humanity, it shall be a social irony. It so happened in the time of Lord Buddha; morality was out of scene. Free inspiration regarding development was under deep pressure. The class, which was required to be a source of inspiration, became instigator of darkness in society as per their deeds. The people of this class began to accord unfair claims on power and privileges. A person from this class could even murder someone and was not liable to be punished. Anyone born in a home belonging to this class automatically controlled other persons. A person of this class was worthy of reverence even if he was characterless. Such were the dictums. A person belonging to that class could commit a sinful act and even then he was patron of religion along with being representative of God. A ***Shudra*** was not authorized to worship freely unto Almighty even if he carried out sublime activities. Such were the moral circumstances. Lord Buddha said on this very account:

"Those cannot be learned who cannot control themselves. They cannot be full of wisdom, who do not make themselves fit according to their education. Those cannot be learned people who cannot engage themselves in sublime activities."

In his own words:

"Attana Evam Pathamam Pathirupe Nivesayam, Athamjamanusayeyaya Na Kilissepya Pandito"

It means, ***"First of all, we should engage ourselves at adequate actions and it is only after that we may accord sermons to others. The learned man can be without disaster only by doing so"***. He also said:

"Attanache Tatha Kapira Yathan-jmanusasati, Sudantovata Dammetha Attahi Kiraduthdhamo"

It means that we should upkeep our conduct in accordance with the sermons, which we are scheduled to pass over to others. We must first control ourselves and only then we should say to others. It is very difficult to control own self. This is a reality. This was a simple but real message of Gautama Buddha. This was amazing and sadly that the regulations framed by a specific class were symbolical of injustice. They were only to sub dice the ***Shudras***. These rules had no need or utility. Truth is ubiquity to us. Why can we not approach a truth straightforwardly? In case God is true, the way to Him should be straightforward. Why God and man cannot meet each other in a direct manner? Persons indulging themselves in evil deeds hide themselves from God under the pretext of religion and its epitaphs. The nature of truthful God cannot be such that someone should be meddling between Him and a human being. When God is real, such distinctions cannot be spiritual and cannot constitute a religion. Only a class cannot be worthy of truthfulness. Why should not people in general be capable of that? All these questions were before Lord Buddha. He announced these queries and said:

"In case it is so, Man does not need such deliberate truth, religion or spirituality, He should refuse such a false conduct."

Lord Buddha negated the unreality of rituals and he held that a society must have clean and developed moral standards because if the moral position of society is inferior [as it was then in human society], any force shall lead only to disaster. Resultantly, political situation shall also be degrading. All evils including causing grief, misutilization, corruption and arbitrariness that can break society shall flourish. In such a situation, the politics shall also be such that will fully turmoil human values. In contradiction, the mental plane of people shall be selfless in case there is adequate moral force in society. The life shall be based on equality and it shall be simple. It will be real and peaceful. Political situation shall also be accessible. It shall be leading to progress. Lord Buddha found society ***'devoid of moral values'***. He also found monarchy to be the centre of misdeeds. Even then he did not attack any religious dogma. He permitted others also to equally march forward. Subsequently, he took upon himself those people in general who were exploited and did not possess rights. He took society towards a simple, practical and real objective.

Lord Buddha did not wish to gain power. He did not need to prescribe complex regulations. He had no reason to impart education of might to his followers. He was well acquainted with the amazing weaknesses of so-called priests. He knew that it was essential in this world to take a human being to a right path. He did this all as a brave warrior and a person of the era who was really mighty. He stressed on human religious establishments and said:

"A hungry person cannot have religion and action. We shall have to fulfill his want in order to get religion and action unto him. As such we cannot control anger also in someone by making him without a want."

He emphasized that it is the religion of a human being to understand first the reality of life. This is the religion of a good order. One who cannot foresee and adopt good religion lives uselessly a life of 100 years. A life of a day is good in case it is full of knowledge of good religion. It means that a person has become familiar with reality of life. In his own words:

"Yo Cha Vassatatam Jeeve Apassam Dhamma Muttam, Ekamha Jivitam Seyoo Passato Dhamma Muttam"

Why after all there is agony in our life? Mahatma Buddha considered it. He deliberated and said:

"Because we are full of selfishness; we are narrow-minded in our thoughts. We work in selfishness. We aspire for personal pleasures and amenities."

He also said:

"We forget humanity while doing so. Result of all these things is bound to be agony. Then what to do? Should we give up soul? Should we consider that there is no rule of God and this deceiving world is at rule? We observe only this world directly. There is no element like soul after the cycle of Birth and Death. It is all a notion. A science subsequently follows other. Every science gets existence within a moment. That very moment that one becomes out of scene. A significant thing is that there is no scientist of science. As such, there is no soul. Body undergoes changes every time. Consciousness and intellect also change in the same manner. As such, soul is dubious dogma which we cherish. Selfishness occurs when we try to remain attached to this dubious spirit of soul. This is the truth. As such, we can be gay if we realize the truth that there is no soul."

Not only that, we shall render happiness unto others. This was Lord Buddha's logical sermon. He himself spent his life in accordance with this sermon.

Lord Buddha stressed on compassion towards every living being and not only towards man. He questioned:

"In case it is good to sacrifice an animal as per slaying, it shall be better to utilize a person in this regard."

He offered himself for such a sacrifice. He considered animal - sacrifice to be very disastrous belief, which was irrational. Lord Buddha said all this emphatically. He prescribed that all are slaves equally to deed and result. What shall be the justification of creation of Universe in case we do not stick to the rule of result as per deed? He refused that ruler is there in some heaven. That ruler may rule as per his wish and may leave us here to suffer agonies.

According to him:

"It is all a lie. Our whole life is perpetual disaster. There is no use of exercising false rituals and different rites etc."

Lord Buddha prescribed that there is only one ideal in the World. All religious-rites are false. We have to discard attachment. After that, only truth shall be in balance. Sun will shine when clouds shall not be there. Do not work towards any misbelief and adopt this principle in total. Sacrifice in real spirit even for the lowest creature. Do not work to please someone or to have an award. Work in order to get salvation through demise of soul. He also said:

"Do not accord regards and worship someone about whom you are ignorant."

Really, Lord Buddha opposed the regulations that were framed for selfish ends on the ground of deceptions and misendeavours. Inhumanity, beastly-ness, poverty and exploitation were the forces of these regulations. These regulations had combined Soul and God. Humanity was destroyed. As such, he undertook real deliberations and explained agony, its cause, its remedy and the ways that were required for this purpose. This explanation grasps the basic tenets of humanity. He called upon to remove the obstacles in the practical aspect of these doctrines through eight middle ways. Middle way i.e., to come out of extreme harshness and simpleness that is not possible.

Eight ways are;

- ***SamyakDrishti ;***
- ***Samyak Vaak;***
- ***Samyak Sankalpa;***
- ***Samyak Vyayaama;***
- ***Samyak Karmanta;***
- ***Samyak Aajivika;***
- ***Samyak Smriti;* and**
- ***Samyak Samadhi***

Mahatma Buddha is a champion of equality. As such, his religion is human-religion. This is directly connected with humanity. Non-violence, Compassion, Sacrifice, alliance, that is friendliness and peace are integrally associated with it.

These are all fundamental and best grounds of human-equality. Above mentioned ingredients must be practiced as far as possible. This will lead to establishment of a human society based on equality. Our way to peace shall be in broader sight.

Lord Buddha considered behaviour to be the foremost. He was one who equated a principle with practice. He was a preacher of a clan in which preachers make a truth, a perfect truth. He presented a burning example while investigating Truth. We shall have to be aware of prime reason behind the calamities that render sufferings unto whole of human-world today. We have ourselves nourished all disasters as per selfishness unto us.

Our old ailment is that of human-distinction. This will have to be finished at all planes: personal, national and international. Spirit of inequality at all levels is basic reason behind evil and turmoil.

The way shown by Lord Buddha is clear. He does not at all compromise with so-called priests. He has no attachment with those with might or with rulers. He does not cherish a man to be a means to misconduct. Lord Buddha did not cherish that a human being should stop before traditions based on misbelieves: to whatever extent old they might be. He did not want that a person should adopt rituals that have been continuing since very long in case they happen to be the means of exploitation. He only wants equal welfare of every human being. This is also foremostly significant and contextual today. We shall make our lives meaningless if we follow the policy of human-exploitation being guided by and having within ourselves spirit of inequality. This is the sermon of Lord Buddha. This is the essence of his peace-oriented human religion.

2. World Religion

Replying to the request by Dr. Paitoon Patyaiying, I said in his class at the PSU, Pattani in 1997:

"Hindu Religious Philosophy incorporates the dictum that religion is what is worth adopting. I agree with this in toto... But what is to be adopted? The answer is goodness. As such, religion consists of adopting goodness. It carries with it the spirit of all-welfare. It may be elaborated thus... Adoption of goodness that leads to all-welfare is a wholesome religion. Its sphere should be broad. It should have total equality."

Christian, Confucian, Zoroastrian, Jain, Buddhist, Islam, Jewish, Sikh and Hindu etc. are taken to be main religions on this earth. ...But, in reality these are not religions. These are religious communities. Each of them directs its followers to lead life in a separate way. This way is based on some eternal value foremostly. This eternal value also incorporates goodness in it. ...But, here the sphere of goodness is not broad because owing to circumstances pertaining to a country and age along with practical position of human beings, this all-welfare does not prove efficacious. It cannot be taken to be complete basis of religion in absence of all's welfare. It is owing to this that it will be apt to take

Hindu, Boddh or Islam ideology based on particular eternal value, to be a religious community while granting it status of an indispensable part of religion. I shall reiterate that scope of religion is vast. It incorporates all-welfare. Equality is ahead of this characteristic. Real universal religion can be established by intermingling fundamental inceptions of all religious communities. This must be done. Happiness and prosperity to all can be possible only through that. One can achieve a state of peace in this world and thereafter [if he or she believes accordingly]. This shall bring an end to all communal differences and all people of the world will be able to be in sphere of fraternity in practice.

As I have already stated, every religious community has a main eternal value. This value is welfaristic. Community emphasizes that it should be derived unto life and explains value for this purpose. It does so in such a manner and through such examples that a man can adopt it in practical life. Forbearance is principal in Hindu Religious Community. It accepts the principle of devoidness of stiffness and accords its followers full opportunity of self-expression. Hindu religious treatises postulate that God is supreme. He has many names. He is forbearing and wants that His offspring, man, should also be forbearing as it leads to self-development. Hindu philosophy combines forbearance with general welfare. It means that man should forbear with inner happiness that there should be welfare of all and all must achieve pleasure and prosperity. ***Rig-Veda*** incorporates as such:

> ***"Asmakama Deva Abhayaya Janmane Sharbhayachchhata Dwipade Chatushpade; Adat Pibadrajayamana Mashitam Tasmemshakar Yorarapom Dadhatana."***[1]

It means:

"O God!, Give pleasure to human beings and beasts all. All creatures may spend life with liberty per getting good food and thereby getting stoutness and energy."

In this manner, there is a desire of welfare of each human being with forbearance. This is the essence of Hinduism.

Bravery is foremost in Sikh Religious Community. It means a struggle for justice and to defend incapables. It is the duty of a Sikh to protect humanity. This is the right path. Sikh ***Gurus*** taught this to their followers through self-practice of this in life. This religious community, which has bravery to be its chief attribute, draws our attention to three significant things:

- ***Nam Simaran*;**
- ***Kirat Karna*; and**
- ***Vand Chhakna*.**

It means:

- To meditate on His name;
- To earn through honest labour; and
- To share with the needy.

This is the essence of this religious community. This is a just path and it aptly cherished; every Sikh has to work for that.

Buddhist Religious Community has compassion as its main attribute. What is compassion? It is to know and take all living beings as friends and by intermingling the spirit of mercy with this friendliness is compassion. It means friendliness and the spirit of mercy are the two pillars of compassion. Lord Buddha called upon us to adopt this heartily and it is also incorporated in...[2] It is not proper to kill any living being... one should desist appreciating anyone who kills some living being... one must oppose killing of any of the all living being-strong or weak.

Buddhist philosophy expects that a friend should urge another to be away from sin and to propagate proper action. Along with that, he should show the way to goodness [religion] and should try to resolve the doubts that others may have. One is really merciful if his deeds, utterances and thoughts are imbued with mercy and he welcomes heartily and is helpful towards fulfillment of our necessities. Such a friend only can be compassionate. It is our duty to adopt spirit of compassion: this is the essence of Buddhist philosophy.

Jain philosophy has non-violence as its main attribute. Probably, no other one stressed on non-violence and explained it explicitly more than Jainism. The making of non-violence is: non+ violence i.e. not to put anyone to violence. It is aptly said, ***"Na himsa is ahimsa"***. Jain philosophy puts, ***"When pain is inflicted unto some other on the level of thought, utterances or deeds, some one's life is taken away, that impure thought, base utterance or non-sacred tendency is considered to be polluted with the evil of violence. It may be outwardly without any sort of violence but the tendency for violence is latent in it."*** The essence is that violence consists in causing misery to anyone by thought, utterance or deed. Contradictory to this all is non-violence. Jain philosophy prescribes three characteristics of violence:

- Misery cause;
- Animosity cause; and
- Misery to self

To apprise human being of humanity, Jain philosophy states:

[A] ***Savvesi Jeeveeyam Peeyam***, which means life is dear to all. Every living being has a very significant will to live. This is a desire that manifests itself up to the moment of death. A living being wishes to live as long as he can. If a man, under condemnation of sentence of death is asked to choose betwixt whole earth and life, he will choose life.

When it is established that all living-beings want to live and no one has accorded us a right to kill him, there should not be unauthorized attempt to worry anyone. In case we do so, others will be trying to revenge on us. Enimity and opposition shall emerge from this point. As such, we must respect right of life unto all and must portray non-violence through our conduct and behaviour.

[B] Panina Cha Piya Daya, which means all living-beings cherish mercy in the same dimension, as they dislike attack on life. Suppose there are two men before an animal of which one has knife in his hand and other one with grass. Seeing both, even the eyes of animal make it clear that he will accept the man with grass in his hand.

As such, it should be the nature of man that he should save lives. Such a grace or mercy inherits fearlessness. One who saves others, himself becomes fearless. Subsequently, he does not apprehend any fear from any living-being. It has been said, ***"Saving gesture is the best of all gestures."*** This also takes us up to epitome of non-violence.

[C] ***Atmavat Sarvabhuteshu***, which signifies realization of pleasures and grief, felt with all the souls in this human world. This realization must be so as if one is himself enjoying pleasure or suffering from that pain. This, after all, leads to good conduct after knowing other one's misery.

[D] ***Parasparopgriho Jivanam***, which clarifies that life of a living being, consists in the righteous action of being mutually cooperative. Meaningfulness of life happens to be in such a gesture. Apt spirit towards others is essence of ***'Humanity'*** and it is also a symptom to identify non-violence.

We may know the meaning of the Grand Religion non-violence by comprehending all these four points. It has been said on this very accord, ***"...Non-violence is very dear Brahman for all living beings. It gives peace."***

To put it:

> "***Ahimsa Savvsattanam Sada Nivveyakarika,***
> ***Ahimsa Savvasattesu Param Bambhamani Diyam***"

Non-violence is non-comparable in itself. The existence of whole world depends upon it. It is essential to adopt it. This is the essence of Jain philosophy.

Jewish Religious Community or Judaism considers justice to be supreme. Justice is supreme in its philosophy. Torah[3] incorporates that Moses said to the People in his 1st speech, ***"Decide judiciously after giving hearance to both the parties, the dispute may be concerning the both from Israel or it may relate to one of the country and another of abroad... Justice knows no favour..."***

This philosophy [Judaism] actually considers justice as the will of God and asks people to live life in accordance with that. Justice fully incorporates equality and fearlessness in it. It must be foremost in human being. It calls upon: Know about exercising' good action, dedicate yourself unto justice... you must favour widows.[4]

This philosophy amply clears good actions. It says that disrespect to elders [including parents], and murder, lust, theft, adultery, false deposition, avarice etc., all are unjust actions. These are not good actions. As such, contradictory to these, respect, security, patronage, truthfulness etc. are virtues towards which we must tend. This is a path to justice and ultimately it happens to be Godly path. God is one. God wants, ***"...All must be dedicated to actions that are just."***

Zoroastrian Religious Community accords unity to humanity. It clearly stipulates that unity is foremost in this ideology. ***'Ahura Mazda'*** is the logic behind this unity:

"He is the Lord of life and knowledge. He is Supreme. He is unified. Compassion, consciousness, justice, love, reality and truthfulness etc., are all his attributes. It is the duty of human being to worship Him alone. All are one because all are His parts. All are equal. No one can be small or big..."

Essence is that all beings are the offspring of one Father and so they themselves should keep unified. They must work with love and cooperation.

This philosophy giving message towards unity states:

"If one is so poor that he has nothing for supper, you should distribute your property amongst poor and

become like that very person if you possess much. This is the way to unity. You will be in grief if you do not do so. As such, be united as all off springs of one Father if you want to save yourself from grief."

This really happens to be the path of peace.

Confucian Religious Philosophy depicts equality as foremost. One, who works with spirit of slavery unto other or takes others to be in his bond, is not a supporter of equality; he is quite antagonistic to humanity. Confucius on this very accord clearly said, ***"Do not behave with others in the manner which you would not like for yourself."***

If a man exploits some one other, it will ultimately give birth to a state of conflict. The society will face divisions and all will go on the path of doom. As such, ***Zen***[5] was made the main basis of his message by Confucius. This is imitable. This is really the essence of Confucius Religious Community.

'Service' is supreme in Christian Religious Community. The First Sermon on the Mount states, ***"He alone is religious who does not have ego and is meek, is full of gentleness, takes things by heart, is religion oriented, merciful, clean and full of spirit of compromise... etc. One, who takes pains in these regards, can only be termed religious."*** Such a religious person that is a person full of above mentioned ideals-engaged in service to humanity, can only be termed as Christian in real sense.

Christianity states, ***"Give plenty unto others but silently. If you extend alms and make publicity of it, it will be inglorious on your part."***

Bible states, ***"... When you give alms, even your left hand should be unaware of what your right hand is doing. Your alms must remain secret."***

Service as portrayed by Christianity is related to self-sacrifice. It may be elaborated in this way that a man should be pure at heart and must keep his word. Along with this, he should be fractural with fellow-beings and should be poised to bring compromise amongst belligerent sides.

A true Christian accords love in exchange of animosity and becomes great only when he vows to serve others. This really remains the aim of life. However, as already emphasized, service must be pure. Purity and impurity, as such, should be clear to us: we should know these terms. As such, it is to be said that Christian Religious Community considers sacrificial service to be supreme. Lord Christ stated at one place, ***"One, who wants to imitate me, must practice self-sacrifice."***[6]

He said at another place, ***"If you want to be perfect, give all of your property to poor."***

The vital point of service in this Religious Community can be understood accordingly.

Fraternity is foremost in Islam. It also considers God to be Supreme and calls upon to tread the way shown by Him. The way God shows is the way to humanity and to serve Him is to serve humanity. Qur'an again and again calls upon people to adhere to fraternity:

"This community [Human] is really one. But they divided themselves on their own."[7]

It means that all human beings happen to be one entity and the difference that is visualized is artificial. It is the duty of man to keep fraternity at top and behave gracefully with parents, relatives, destitute and poor. He must talk only what is good must inspire ***Namaz*** and must give ***Zakat.***[8]

Prophet Mohammad's life is a very good example pertaining to fraternity. He always kept it uppermost in his thoughts and actions. There are innumerable examples in ***Hadis*** in this regard. It is said:

"My love has become essential for those who love each other owing to me, sit together owing to me, meet each other and spend on each other."[9]

The substance is that we must accept existence and authority of God and should have faith in Him. Mutual cooperation and affection is necessary for this. ***Hadis*** states in this chain, ***"If a man loves another, it is ashelovesGod"***[10]

Prophet Mohammad says, ***"Speaking sweet and giving food to hungry is the Islam."*** Therefore, People should have mutual relations for the sake of God. We should love each other. More than that... ***"A Momin [Muslim] is abode of love. That person is not gentle who does not love any one and whom no one loves."***[11] Such a person cannot be Mohammedan. Evidently, Islam presents the best example of fraternity. It can be termed in following words - Fraternity is main attribute in Islam.

It is clear from above discussion that one eternal value is supreme in every religious community. The related religious community asks its followers to lead life on the basis of this value in order to get pleasure, prosperity and peace. It is aimed at fulfillment of their life. As such, the motive of every religious community is identical All eternal values are complementary to each other. As such, there cannot be a state of conflict.

Of course, there is a necessity to grasp basic principles of every religious community. To this purpose, there must be a committee above all religious communities and that committee should establish coordination amongst fundamental principles of all communities [because principles and values are complementary to each other] and must make people in this world understand that these are not contradictory. Ultimately, all have a common goal. Motive of all is one. Ways to achieve the goal- method of worship and rituals etc. may be different but motive is one. This purpose is to obtain ultimate aim along with pleasure and prosperity. This committee will, as such, establish a world-religion while carrying out above-mentioned functions. This world religion is essential: it is the need of the hour.

References

1. ***Rig-Veda*,** 10:3:37:11
2. ***Dharma Aur Vishwa-Shanti***, 2nd [E] Edition, 1997, p.51
3. Religious Book of Jews
4. ***Isaiah***, 1:17
5. Humanity
6. New Testament [H], p.28
7. ***Qur'an*** [H], S.2, p.1
8. Same as above, S.2, p.1
9. ***Hadis*** [H], p.145
10. Same as above, p.324
11. As above p.336

3. Role of Religion in Human Life

What a childishness those people display who try to subdue or deny the role of religion in human life, or even brand religion as unnecessary. Throughout the world, I myself have come across many such people who deny the role of religion in human life saying that it is unnecessary. A young friend of mine from Odense city in Denmark even wrote a letter to me on this subject and quoted the sayings of Karl Marx.[1]

Actually the use of words like unnecessary, unimportant etc. is not new in respect of religion. I have heard such words used with religion, right from my childhood. I have also been listening to the explanation that the users of such words give. I remember .the statement of a gentleman where he said, ***"Religion is the biggest obstacle in the path of human development."***

To be candid, I myself regarded religion as unnecessary for quite some period during my childhood and youth. I even agreed with the statement of Karl Marx, although I had no knowledge regarding its meaning, purpose and the thousands of years old history.

As I said a short while ago, I remember very well the explanations given by people who regard religion as unnecessary, unimportant and only a personal issue and an obstacle in the path of progress. A well known scholar of the last century had stated casually, ***"... Before engaging in religion etc., human being needs food, clothing and shelter."***[2] Many scholars have made such statements in the past as well in this century.

Certainly, there is no need to elaborate the importance of food, clothing, shelter and other basic needs in human life. We all know and understand the extent to which man can go in order to fulfill these basic needs. So if someone reasons that in the absence of bread for food, clothes to wear and roof for shelter, what is the meaning and benefit of getting involved in religion? It is but natural that knowingly or unknowingly, people without food, clothing and shelter will lean towards the above mentioned reasoning.

Today the population of this world is above 6000 million and a major portion of this population is deprived of the bare minimum basic necessities, as such this deprived class will lean towards explanations given against the role, utility and necessity of religion, irrespective of the fact whether there is any truth behind these explanations or not.

The fact is that the eminent personalities or scholars who diminish or deny the role of religion in human life by using words like unimportant, unnecessary or obstacle in the path of progress, are not very honest while doing so. They alienate themselves from truth. That is why their statements and explanations appear childish to me. Actually by using the above mentioned words they mean to refer to religious communities but while doing so they assume both religion and religious community to be one although both[3] are distinct from each other in terms of their meaning, purpose, scope and historical background. The above-mentioned eminent people and scholars do not concentrate on this context. It need not be said that the arguments that they are supposed to use only in terms of religious communities; the discussion that should be done only in case of religious communities, they do so about religion too. By doing so they are doing injustice not only to the subject but to their own erudition too. No doubt, religion and religious communities are distinct from each other not only in terms of their meaning but also in terms of establishment, purpose and scope. In terms of chronology [history] there is a big difference between the two. Therefore, it is not reasonable to comment on the necessity, importance or role of religion without factual knowledge about it. If someone tries to do so, it would certainly be his childishness.

Thousands of years ago, human life began at one place. During that period, various parts of the earth were joined together which separated with the passage of time. Whatever exists within the scope of our ability to see and understand is subject to constant change. The Earth, other planets and satellites or any object in this universe are no exceptions to this. The various parts of the earth today are not in the same condition as they were in the past. And in the future they will not remain as they are today. So from one-place human beings spread throughout the earth by creating a conducive environment for progress.

You are well aware of the fact that many scholars believe in the transition of apes to man. I do not agree with the Darwinian or let's say agreements of the followers of Darwinian Theory regarding human evolution, although, I admire the well thought, cleverly presented the so called convincing arguments put forth in the above mentioned theory. But this is not our point of discussion here.

I firmly believe that religion was with man from the beginning of his life. This is in his nature, though it is an entirely different matter that he realized it while thinking about the security of his existence. When the thought materialized into reality, the position of religion became clear. How? We will understand by knowing the meaning of religion.

Religion- the ***dharma***, in its broad meaning is Goodness and adoption.[4] As human being was born with the great value of non-violence, we can definitely say that religion was with him right from the birth and as already indicated, he realized this during his struggle to secure his existence. As soon as he realized it, he started living a more stable life as a community with others.[5] By doing this, not only his, but other's existence too became secure. Truly, religion is dedicated to welfare of all and thus its scope is extensive. We should remember that all goodness that is linked for the welfare of all is religion. To absorb goodness is religion, today and in the future too. It was so in the past too.

I had said that non-violence is a permanent feature of mankind. Many people might not agree with this statement. I would like to humbly request these people to think as to what might have happened if non-violence had not been a part of human beings. No doubt in the beginning itself, man would have become nonexistent.

Generally what we consider religion is in fact religious community. Religious communities are many not one. They were established in different periods under different circumstances and requirements on different parts of the earth. For example thousands of years ago, ***Vedic*** Religious Community was, established in Asia. Similarly, 2000 years ago Christianity in Israel and 1400 years ago Islam in Arabia came into existence, In India, the ***Sikh*** Religious Community came into existence about 500 years ago.

I believe that the founders of religious communities gave a new direction to human life style keeping in mind the immediate future and contemporary point of view. They also made many eternal values a basis of direction out .of which one remained principal.

Certainly directions shown by each religious community are different, even if their goal eventually is the same. It is natural that out of many directions some will be suitable to some people and not to the rest it is not possible that a single one be suitable to all. Thus what is not suitable to all, cannot bring welfare to all. Such directions cannot be religion. Yes, it can be religious community. Thus, religion is superior to any religious community. This is what needs to be understood.

I cannot agree that human welfare was not the motive behind the establishment of religious communities by the establishers although their scope might be limited. But it is ironic that the followers of these religious communities diverged from the basic aim, feeling or values and using it as a shield exploited fellow human beings. Various inhuman deeds were perpetrated. They even divided their own religious communities into various sects and gave them the name of '***religion***'. You will find that majority of religious communities have two or more sects. Is this in accordance with the feelings of the establishers of religious communities? Not at all.

Our history testifies to the occurrence of numerous upheavals and wars in the name of religious communities.

We only need to look at 11th century's European history. We see that the so-called stalwarts of religious communities themselves caused many riots and wars. I am sure many of you are aware of them. My indication is towards the many religious wars or crusades.

Let me take you a little back in history. About 500-600 B. C., in the Indian region, you will find that the ***Vedic*** people in contrast to the basic value[6] and practice of their religious community, indulged in many inhuman activities. They were involved in activities of inequality and exploitation. While using religious community as a shield clearly they were misusing their religious community. This was the period when Gautama Buddha was born. Did the fundamental or principal value of ***Vedic*** Religious Community have anything to do with these inhuman acts? Not at all! I can give numerous such examples not only in the Indian context but on a global scale as well. This happens even today. You hear about it now and then. But still I will firmly state that it is against the fundamental basis of religious communities and that unspeakable inhuman acts have been perpetrated under the shield of religious community.

All this has happened is happening and possibly will happen in the future too. But what is shocking for you and me is that the scholars have linked these atrocities with religion itself and are still doing it today. Many scholars have ignored the difference between religion and religious communities and belittled religion by branding it irrelevant and denied its role in human life whereas religion has always been committed to general welfare and will remain so in the future. In these belittled interpretations, sect and sub-sects too are considered to be religion. Is this not their ignorance?

Religion is much superior to religious community. Religion is committed to general welfare. It was needed not only in the beginning periods of human beings, but today also it is needed. It was important not only during the beginning for surety of existence and later in development but is important today also. It urges for unity and cooperation to build a conducive environment and to solve day-to-day problems. Whoever has become familiar with its reality has understood its meaning; will always adopt a feeling of co-operation.

Not only this, he will be dedicated to unity and he will not face the day-to-day problems. This is how great the role of religion in human life is. If we want to be trouble free, move towards real progress, attain peace then we not only have to understand religion but accept its role in life too.

References

1. Regarding religion being opium.
2. Angles quoting Marx.
3. Religion and religious-communities.
4. *Dharma Dharyate Iti.*
5. Who had similar realization.
6. Forbearance.

4. Necessity of Religion*

I vividly remember that day of August 1998 when Maothong asked me, ***"What is the necessity of religion?" i.e. "Can't we live without religion?"*** Although Maothong's pertinent question urged me to give a prompt reply then and there, but I thought it would be inappropriate to do so. That's why I told her, ***"I will answer your question on my forthcoming visit to the campus. Please wait until then."*** Now again after 10 months, I have an opportunity to be present amongst you. Maothong is also present here. I would like to answer the question briefly by citing a real example. But before that I would like to clarify those points that according to me are at the root of the question.

First of all, the question that Maothong asked regarding ***'necessity of religion'*** was in fact related to religious community. Religion and religious community, both, differ in their meaning, subject, scope etc. It is possible for you and me to be members of different religious communities and at the same time be adherents of the same religion. Therefore it is imperative for all of us, students of religion and philosophy, to get well acquainted with the meaning, subject, scope etc-.of religion and religious community.

Secondly, Maothong was repulsed by certain inhuman acts that were perpetrated under the cover of religious community. This repulsion created anguish. I believe that's why she had asked the question. I request you to understand the establishment of a religious community, the reality of its goals and the circumstances also. By doing so, you will become aware of the real situation. You will be able to reconsider the anguish caused by the above-mentioned repulsion.

And, thirdly, you should be aware that one could terminate one's affiliation with a religious community; one can even change one's religious community. All over the world, there are many, who are not a part of any religious community. This is their personal matter. Contrary to this, one is always attached with religion. It is almost impossible to separate oneself from religion Therefore your question is unreal. Convert it into a real one by amending, ***"What is the necessity of religion?"*** To ***"What is the necessity of religious community?"***

II

After clarifying the three points mentioned above, I would like to give an authentic example as I have stated in the beginning. It occurred about 52 years back. A country was divided on the basis of two religious communities. As a result there was large scale migration of population from one part to another and along with that, there was looting and innumerable incidents of inhuman atrocities. Violence was the worst that included mass inhuman massacre of the innocents.

Amidst this chain of events, in a village, two families with a total of eleven members could not migrate with people of their own community in time. As a result around midnight they were surrounded by a group of fanatics of the opposite community who locked the houses of both families from outside and started preparing to loot them and kill them by burning down their houses. According to their plan, majority of them went to their home to fetch kerosene and other materials. Only four or five persons were left to guard the families. The helpless people locked inside the houses, awaited their end with bated breath. Suddenly for some unknown reason, the men guarding the house threw open the doors, probably to know what the people inside were doing. There might be some other reason too, behind the doors that were opened.

Now there were eleven people inside and only four or five outside, those too were not physically sturdy. Thus making use, of the opportunity, the family members pushed aside the guards and made good their escape. But soon the fanatics regrouped. Those who had gone to fetch kerosene etc. had returned.

The eleven family members now fled for their lives with the fanatics hot in pursuit. There was a church about half a kilometer from the village. Father Thomas was in charge and Sister Elizabeth, a model of selfless service, lived along with him. That day father was not present at the church. The main door of the church was open. Sister was peacefully reading ***'The Sermon on the Mount"***[1], and meditating on each word that she read. Suddenly, eleven people rushed in through the already open door of the church. Sister was quick to realize that those people had arrived, in order to save their lives.

Immediately ***'sister'*** applied the message of ***'Faith in God'***, heartily. She stood up and closed the main door from inside. She took the eleven members towards the back of the church and sealed them in a chamber. After that she again continued studying the Holy Bible.

The murderous crowd following the families reached the church. They knocked at the door. Sister opened the door. Many from the crowd shouted:

"Where are they?"
"Who?" Sister enquired nonchalantly.
"The same people who came running this way."
"...But nobody came here. I was reading the Bible all by myself..." .
"So nobody came here?"
"No, nobody at all."
"Do you swear by the Bible?"

Sister was well aware of the admonition given by Lord Jesus in his '***Sermon***' regarding taking '***oath***'[2] without delay, silently she touched the Bible to her forehead. The crowd went back. Eleven lives were saved. Let me tell you that the eleven people who were saved were not Christians i.e. they did not belong to sister's religious community. Moreover, the fanatics who were intent on killing and looting them were not Christians either.

By keeping complete faith in God and touching the Bible to her forehead, Sister Elizabeth saved not one but eleven lives that did not belong to her religious community. What do we call this? Certainly this was an exercise of carrying out her religious duty. In the definition of religion, '***Goodness'*** is to be adopted. At that time, it was '*good*' for Sister Elizabeth to save the lives of eleven humans. This was her religion and she carried it out properly and beautifully.

Religion is above the religious community. Its scope is extensive and involves welfare of all. Contrary to this, religious community is limited and is below religion. Even if you are not affiliated with any religious community, but if you claim to be a human being you cannot disassociate yourself from religion. Religion is the essential condition for both humanity and existence. The reason is clear. If goodness, which is the definition of religion, is not complete; then what will be the consequences? You can well understand. Therefore, we cannot rule out the necessity of religion under any circumstance. The only requirement is that you understand it properly.

I agree that no religious community, in its original form, obstructs the path of religion. It is even helpful in carrying out one's religious duties. Sister Elizabeth was a good Christian. She adopted the teachings and the principal value[3] of Christian Religious Community. That is why she had risen to the level where and when it was required; she was able to carry out her duties. Had she not been a good Christian, I suspect she probably would have failed in carrying out her religious duties. But sister did not fail and she did the ***'good'*** work of saving lives.[4]

It is true that under the veil of religious communities, many inhuman acts were perpetrated. Mankind was thrown into the flame of violence. There are not one but many instances to prove the above. Even then, shall I believe that any religious community would really encourage its adherents to commit inhuman acts or violence? I cannot believe so. Why? Because I am well aware of the aim behind the establishment of religious communities and the circumstances involved. I know that needs in particular periods of time, gave birth to religious communities for the welfare of specific human communities. This was thought over by one or more than one great personage, saint or reincarnate and keeping the best possible values, under the existing circumstances, chiefly in mind, urged the people to model their day to day activities in accordance with that.

I request you not to be distracted by one or two incidents that were inhuman and were committed under the cover of religious community.

Do not foster hatred for religious community either. Do not let anguish develop inside you. As already mentioned, religious communities are not devoid of a person behind their establishment. How good it will be if we become true adherents of our religious community i.e., adopt its teachings fully and then proceed in the field of religion and make ourselves adaptable there also. This is what is really needed.

References

1. In his ***'Sermon on the Mount'***, Lord Jesus urged to have Faith in God and thus have no worries.
2. Lord Jesus has warned man regarding taking ***Oath*** in any manner, in his ***'Sermon on the Mount'***.
3. Service.
4. It is mentioned in the New Testament that Lord Jesus said, "...***You are the light of this world... let your light shine in such a manner that on seeing your good work they praise your heavenly father [God]."***

5. War and Peace in Relation to Religion*

Prior to viewing War and Peace in relation to Religion, it would be better if we first understand the meaning of religion. What is religion? As I have already clarified in my lecture delivered in various countries, ***'Religion is to adopt goodness.'*** This religion had its origin on this planet along with human being. That is both were born together. Religion is devoted or dedicated to welfare of one and all. Its scope is very wide. If it had not been with human being from the very beginning then what to say of progress made by him so far, his very existence would have been extinct. So it is necessary that we understand well the real or true meaning of religion. It is owing to the fact that usually or generally religious community is considered as religion that is not fair or proper. Religion and religious community are quite different.

Understanding and persuading the meaning of religion in context of adopting goodness, we have to magnify the discussion on ***'War and Peace.'***

War and Peace are, in reality, two different situations in which one leads us towards decay and destruction and the other towards welfare. The basis of war is violence while the basis of peace is non-violence. Non-violence is in human nature permanently. It is in itself a religion, realization of which was made by man in the very beginning. I mean, first of all.

Violence is the contradictory situation of non-violence. It can never come within the circumference of sanctity. Why is it so? It is because whatever is gained on its basis is not at all sacred, stable or permanent. Someone may give an argument against this statement or my point of view but I am firm on my opinion. I know that violence is ever an impure mean.

Not only one but several instances come before us which reveal that in order to end injustice, when there was no other alternative left except to use violence, it was recoursed to. In other words, violence was used as the alternative or means. By using this, triumph was achieved. But definitely we shall have to agree that even then it was not within the domain of sanctity. I can stress on it firmly in relation to wars fought in presence of propounders of religious communities or their leaders.

Hindus have two great ideals. These are Lord Rama and Lord Krishna. In the times of both of them terrible and fiercest; wars were fought. Rama straight way, fought with Ravana- the then king of Lanka. It was in the nature of a world war. Numerous lives were lost and property was damaged. As described, Rama was fighting for justice. It is also described that before indulging in the war, he adopted various non-violent measures so as to remain aloof from or avoid nude dance of violence. But when no alternative, within the sphere of non-violence could be successful, he had to resort to violence.

He became victorious. But as a human being, he also imbibed in him the virtue of non-violence. So the remnants of pain for countless people killed in the fiercest battle, subsisted in his heart. We can realize this pain in Rama, after the war, in his following request to Indra:

"Sunu Surupati Kapi Bhaloo Hamare,
Pare Bhoomi Nisicharanahi Je Mare,
Mama Hita Lagi Taje Inha Prana,
Sakal Jiao Sures Sujana"

Meaning thereby:

"Listen O king of heaven! Our monkeys and bears are lying there on the ground. They have laid their lives... restore them all life, wise Lord of gods!"

During Lord Krishna's time ***Mahabharata*** was fought like world war. As described, Krishna was guiding or pioneering the side indulged in war for justice. People having knowledge of ***Mahabharata*** know that there is mention in it that ***'Non-violence is religion in grandeur.'*** It is also mentioned that Lord Krishna has himself stated that even if any one non-violent way is available... we should give up violence and adopt the non-violent way. But as it is said; in order to wipe off injustice, there was no other alternative left except a recourse to violence. Consequently, battle of ***Mahabharata*** took place. Hundreds of thousands of people were killed; dreadful destruction was displayed. Probably not a single sphere was left which would not have destroyed. Lord Krishna's side became victorious. But he never hailed the terrible consequences that ensured in the wake of war. ***'Had God willed otherwise'***, it was the call from the core of his heart.

Likewise, there are several examples, not only in the Hindu Religious Community but also in those of other religious communities. I do not want to dwell on them at length at this juncture. I only want to stress that non-violence is permanently in human nature; ultimately he realizes it. And it is the only reason that after violence, a time certainly comes when human heart spontaneously speaks, ***'Had God willed otherwise'*** or ***'Had it never occurred'.***

History is full of numerous instances relating thereto. Here, I shall present only one example that is about Emperor Ashoka [3rd Century B.C.]. Ashoka fought the war with the king of the state of Kalinga. In the battle, about one hundred thousand people were killed. Far more people than this number were injured and one hundred fifty thousand were made prisoners. I have no data concerning the loss of property. As is known, Ashoka became victorious. But soon he had the futility from violence. He felt deep sorrow at the nude dance of violence. He followed the way of compassion. Although he, throughout his life, had recourse to the path of compassion but the big empire set up by he was founded on the basis of violence. All know that his empire did not last long.

And why only about Ashoka, how far did the big empires extend on the basis of war, could continue to remain in permanent existence? Where are they in existence today? So, I stress that violence can never come within the sphere of sanctity. Whatever is achieved on its strength; can never remain stable.

Contrary to it, everything achieved through non-violence is ever abiding, permanent and sacred. Man realized it when he was tempted to the safety of his existence, although it was already in his nature from his very origin. Thus it was the only first religion for the surety of his life, the realization of non-violence and thereafter its continuous development was the greatest need. That is why, all religious communities, founded later on, gave a foremost place to it in their values. None of the prophets, propounders or saints made its importance less. How could they afford to do so? It is very essential for the achievement of peace. And peace is the aim of human life. It is only in it that progress is possible. What anyone will gain from war? What will be achieved by causing destruction? Let us ponder over it. Let us keep aloof from violence, the basis of war, and give preference to the non-violence - the basis of peace. And while doing so remember the past wars. If not much, we should not at least forget the colossal amount of loss of lives and property the last two world wars of this century brought about.

In many of my lectures and also in writings, I have tried to mention about loss that took place during the last two world wars. On the basis of available data, I have stated that in the First World War one ***crore*** [ten million] and in the other World War five ***crore*** [fifty million) people were killed. In the first one about 2.25 ***crore*** and in the second nearly 3.5 ***crore*** of people were severely wounded. A few days ago, I have seen and known these data extensively or in detail, particularly relating to First World War, have confirmed that one ***crore*** people killed in First World War were known dead soldiers only. Besides, 30 ***lakhs*** presumed dead soldiers were also there. Not only this, one crore thirty ***lakhs*** civilians were killed; ninety ***lakhs*** people were orphaned; fifty *lakhs* became widows. As I have already stated, out of entire population 1225 millions were badly affected; their condition became pitiable. The number of refugees was one crore and that of prisoners was thirty ***lakhs***.

This is the situation. Now, I leave it to you to ponder over it. What war can bring to mankind? Nothing. So please come and join me to declare that we shall avoid violence - the basis of war, continuously, admitting that war is inherently and essentially a supreme violation of Jesus' way of life and Christianity.

6. Zoroastrianism: A View

"Only one Ahura Mazada[1] there is. He is Lord of life and knowledge...He is Supreme and is epitome of ultimate peace. He is one and only one. Consciousness, Truth, Justice, Reality, Love and Compassion emerge only as per His being. Man should worship Him and may peace be unto man."

The propounder of Zoroastrian Faith –Spitama Zoroaster's above mentioned dictum accords unity of humanity and thereby puts a human being as a ***bead in rosary***: the rosary can be compared to world peace. As we are already in the knowledge of single God theory of total faith in such a Divine system, this philosophy enunciates whole humanity to be part of God. All being his part happen to be equal. No one should be termed big or small. All must worship Him and should try to be His achiever: this only is state of peace.

Spitama Zoroaster was born about two thousand B.C. in ***Aryan*** Clan in Southern Iran. A social and religious condition was full of utter complexities at that time. Man was under darkness of sanctimoniousness then. He was extremely involved in sacrificing animals in names of gods and in other forms. There existed an evil of Black Magic and every human being was sad owing to that. Many social evils were stated to be right under the name of religion. Intoxication had also been one of the evils. There was darkness at individual, social and national planes. Man was victim of non-peace. He was sad and was surrounded by difficulties.

Zoroaster experienced all this at an early age. He began to ponder over this grief when he was only fifteen years of age. He gave up worldly pleasures, which actually happened to be the cause of grief and turmoil, and began to pursue peace. He became twenty after five years and now after denunciating home, he began to think deeply of taking abode in a cave. He continued to think in this manner for ten years and ultimately he gained knowledge at the age of thirty. [3] Subsequently, he began to tread path of peace and as a Prophet imparted message for the peace of world.

What is the message? How can we get real pleasure after getting rid of grief and can be able to establish peace in the world? Towards this, Zoroaster put the most significant fact of oneness of human beings before us. He prescribed that we all are offspring of single God. No one can be our master except God. As such, human beings must learn to be united with love and cooperation. In other words, he took human unity to be supreme and stated single God purview to be the basis of this. This is really a very important and handsome step in the direction of establishment of world peace. In addition to that, other significant messages in Zoroastrian philosophy for this purpose are:

True Actions

Zoroaster said about two types of actions:

- True; and
- False.

Every human being happens to be in the midst of true and false both. This can be compared to a bridge in the midst of two banks. A bridge separates two banks as well as it unites them. In the same way, man can separate true and false actions and can also bring them together. In case a man aspires for prosperity and state of peace, he must indeed tend towards true actions. This remains to be full of goodness and attributes of welfare. In his very words:

"Pleasure, peace, disaster...all results from good [truthful] or bad [false] deeds of man."

He also gave a message that one can be near to God by true actions only. This also indicates existence of humanity. It clearly means that man's existence depends upon true actions. As such, a man will have to perform true actions if he aspires for peace. False action is at the root of grief.

Liberality and Fraternity

Zoroaster emphasized liberality and fraternity along with human unity. His highly remarkable and real message was:

"In case a man adopts fraternity in real sense and keeps a pace with liberal policy along with that, he gives himself unto that spirit of equality which is liked by his God and which imparts peace to him."

He not only gave this message but applied it in his practices and, as such, presented very good examples before human world. In Zoroastrian treatises, there is a good episode in this context and it can be cited as an example here. According to it, there had been a very severe famine on earth in the age of Zoroaster. All were under its attack. Grief of already grief-stricken became unbound. Many of them died. His parents were wealthy and so he urged them to distribute all amongst poor and depressed. His parents did so. Everything was distributed. Now, the family of Zoroaster became equally poor. This was a unique example of liberality, fraternity and equality. He continued to impart this very message throughout his life; it was not an act limited to message giving alone-he treated this path practically in life.

Liberty

A man in chains can never prosper in any field of life. Not only can that, a dependent one, cannot develop him spiritually. It is on this count that Zoroastrian philosophy highly applauded human liberty. Topics related to human liberty have been there more than once in *Avesta*[3] and in all of them he has been accorded right to this. To quote one of them:

"Man is free in this world to know darkness and light, good and bad; justice and injustice and truth and non-truth. He is at liberty to understand and adopt good or bad. God Himself granted this freedom to man. But as we get a handsomely good fruit in future if we sow a handsomely good plant at present, in the same way-the actions carried out with the spirit of fairness, justice and truth accord us prosperity and peace. It is the duty of man to know this and act accordingly. This is the way of enlightenment."

Human liberty has really been given foremost position in Zoroastrian philosophy. Liberty has been preferred not only in worldly practices but also in sphere of *summon bonoum* that is ultimately good sphere. It has been described:

"Almighty want His offspring to be near Him...but with self-will and affectionately."

Mercy and Friendliness

Man should have the spirit of mercy not only towards man but unto every living being and this mercy must imbibe itself with the spirit of friendliness-Zoroaster called upon this humanity in his message. Mercy and friendliness together constitute compassion. Compassion occupies important place in eternal human values. It was on this account that Zoroaster declared as inhuman the customs of sacrifice and violence prevalent in his times and also declared them to be symbolic of non-peace. He declared:

"Mercy and friendliness are indicative of humanity. Man cannot be perfect in the absence of them."

In this way, Zoroaster called upon man to imitate the way to peace while imparting into him knowledge of eternal human values like liberty, mercy, friendliness, fraternity, truthfulness and equality. Who can deny that these eternal values shall not bring all-sided development to man and will not promise position of peace unto him? It is, of course, imperative that behaviour should be conducted in accordance with these values :

"Good, that is-sacred thought, good words and talks and good actions of sacred nature are necessary to achieve this ambition."

This is the purpose-cum-meaning of the main principles in Zoroastrian philosophy: ***Humata, Hukta, Huvarashta* or *Manashmi, Gavashmi* and *Kunashmi***

Zoroastrian philosophy incorporates active goodness as the most important point. This philosophy aims at making all-sided development of man who can be termed well as per above mentioned main values and Godly grace. A man, so all-sided developed, can only be considered prosperous. This is all we can say in brief about Zoroastrianism.

References

1. God.
2. Like Lord Buddha and ***Tirthankara*** Mahavira's thoughts, main thing in Spitama's thought was to know about the mystery. This relates to questions as to why there is misery in the World. Why death...? Why are some oppressed and hungry, whereas others are rich and prosperous? Why any evil, whatsoever, cropped in this world? Etcetera
3. ***Avesta*** is the main religious treatise of Zoroastrian philosophy.

7. Hiinayaana Motivation of Self-Beginning for Welfare

Generally, it is believed that the ***Hiinayaana*** one of the prominent schools of thoughts of Buddhism is individualistic. Maximum stress of ***Hiinayaana*** is to take humans towards happiness and salvation or liberation from his personal sufferings. Some have also extended an argument that because ***Hiinayaana*** philosophy is centralized upon individual, it is micro in dimension; and it is for this reason perhaps that it has been linked to word ***'hiina'***, which in simple words can be translated to ***'lesser'***, ***'small'*** or ***'low'***. But in reality, despite being centralized on individualism, the message and objective of ***Hiinayaana*** philosophy is neither small nor its depth can be underestimated; especially because not only in the East, rather Western scholar like Gene Hopp also agrees that ***"Hiinayaana Buddhism is a good introduction [itself] of Buddhism what the Buddha [himself] taught".***

Thus, reality is that ***Hiinayaana*** philosophy was in existence even before the ***Mahaayaana***, another prominent branch of Buddhism; may be not in the name of ***Hiinayaana***, because nomenclature ***Hiinayaana*** came to light at the time of rising of ***Mahaayaana*** during a broad philosophical discourse on Buddhist philosophy, which took place after Lord Buddha. Nevertheless, ***Hiinayaana*** was discovered as a rival word by a great intellectual belonging to the ***Mahaayaana*** school of thought. May be or may not be that great intellectual might have meant to downgrade its rival philosophy in comparison to their own views and for this reason he called it ***Hiinayaana*** [lesser vehicle]. Even then, ***Hiinayaana*** is not a lesser vehicle; as it is important and relevant even today.

As is well known, Lord Buddha also accepted the principle of enjoying or suffering the consequences of one's actions. He agreed that humans are liable to the destiny according to one's deeds. Buddha declared the human deeds as the reason of repeated birth-death and rebirth and accepted deed itself as the basis of ultimate salvation. The principle of four noble truths [***dukha***-suffering, source of ***dukha***, cessation of ***dukha*** and the path of cessation of ***dukha***] expounded by him, firstly shows the fact [mirror] of human life and then provides point wise knowledge and intelligence to make it purposeful and fruitful. Not only has this, Lord Buddha's call for determined adaptation and specific commitments and promises for development of ideal virtues, especially ***shila***-the moral conduct [which is literally linked to calmness and pleasantness], also started virtually from individual life.

Shila turns a person virtuous and for this reason Lord Buddha has laid so much stress on it. A virtuous person can exercise self-control and then as a key to all happiness and dedicated to goodness, one can reach to the entire depths of the nature of excellent conduct. He can progress on the path of salvation of self and then of entire universe.

In reality, one can start from self. By renunciation of evils, a person, while developing ideal virtues through his good deeds, leads on the path of self welfare and reaches the stage of salvation; establishes himself as ideal for others and then inspires others towards that path [of salvation]. An individual who is not able to proceed on the path of self-welfare and reach the ultimate can not become ideal or inspiration for others. This is the universal truth. Beginning shall have to be made from the bottom; that is, from the level of individual. This is the crux of teachings of ***Hiinayaana.*** It contains the condition of becoming light for welfare of self first. ***Hiinayaana*** message is to show enormous light to others after making the self-luminous and shinning.

8. Non-Violence: A Natural, Dynamic and Live Value

Non-violence, that is ***ahimsa***, is not a rough thing, nor is it an inactive thought or a value established by man. Non-violence is a natural, dynamic, active or live value. Because of its permanent existence in human nature, its being dynamic and active non-violence is an essential condition for existence, development and the ultimate goal, and for this very reason it is the first and absolutely necessary base of civilization.

Best manifestation of non-violence took place in Lord Mahavira. For Mahavira non-violence is the soul-force. Besides being nucleus in Jain philosophy, the form of non-violence that shaped in his individual practices and daily routine, nevertheless, it did not exist in the life of any of his contemporaries. It this regard Mahavira is unparallel even today; and after him anybody equaled him or has been able to follow him completely, is beyond my knowledge and belief.

Further for Gautama Buddha, and in modern times, for Mahatma Gandhi, non-violence is, ultimately, a natural value. As for many incarnations, prophets, philosophers and thinkers, since ancient to modern times, for Buddha and

Gandhi also it is the principal human value. Although Gautama Buddha did not directly accept the naturalness of non-violence, but the manner in which he has repeated love for life as innate desire by all ***[Sabbes Jeeviyam Piyam]***, and disliking for violence and punishment ***[Sabbe Tashanta Dandassa]***, the conclusion is drawn that non-violence is a natural value. Buddha laid stress on maximum purity in daily practices and he called for practical non-violence as much as possible. For this reason, non-violence became the subject of more and more practices in his philosophy.

Mahatma Gandhi's arguments that ***'man has made consistence progress in direction of non-violence' and in a natural way 'mankind moved towards non-violence for progresses'*** spontaneously confirm the naturalness of this value from his side also. For Gandhi too, non-violence is the subject of maximum practices and ultimately its yardstick is the intention behind the action. According to Mahatma Gandhi, importance lies in making non-violence conducive to circumstances of time and space; it is the base on which success of non-violence depends. No doubt, this conception towards non-violence is acceptable to all-general or particular.

Non-violence of Mahavira is the soul-force whereas non-violence of Buddha and Gandhi is a natural value. By speaking so, readers may presume that there is a difference in views of Mahavira, Buddha or Gandhi regarding non-violence. In other words, there is a difference between above-mentioned concepts relating to non-violence in which it soul-force according to Mahavira, while it is a natural value according to Buddha and Gandhi. But in reality it is not so. Definitely soul reflects the nature, or we can say that nature is influenced by soul. Therefore, the one that is the soul-force is, more or less, natural also.

So far as the question of non-violence being dynamic and live or an active value is concerned, in that Mahavira, Buddha, Gandhi and many other also, are unanimous. Let us now have some discussion regarding non-violence being a dynamic and active value.

As historical evidences confirm, in its primitive age man adopted the technique of living and stabilizing together. By doing so, man showed co-operation towards fellow man, which, like affection, is another supplementary value of non-violence. And interestingly, even in primitive age, after mutual co-operation humans did not make a final stop. Man did not stop satisfied at the feeling of his own safety and that of his contemporaries. On the contrary he had a keen desire to move forward. In other words, man was crazy enough to further develop the sense of mutual co-operation. And this was the reason that he continuously co-operated with others and established new records, one after the other. Because of this natural instinct man is still on the path of progress and he has to go further and further. Despite the presence of many hurdles, worldly competitions and envy, the instinct of co-operation with others could not elope from human nature and it will never elope. Because of this instinct man will remain active as far as possible, he shall continue to proceed towards prosperity.

Not on the strength of any theory, but on the basis of day-to-day practices and self-experiences, any one can reach the conclusion that non-violence and non-violent activities, and mainly co-operation, increases further with more efforts; it becomes conducive to us. Therefore, it can be emphatically said that non-violence is dynamic besides being an active value. Needless to say that non-violence is in our nature and it has the capacity to consistently develop.

Any one who has least doubt in the activeness of non-violence or its dynamism, he can remove doubt by experiences of worldly practices of his own and others. There can be no question mark on non-violence being an active, dynamic and natural value.

Natural, active and dynamic value non-violence is entirely linked to heroism, or in other words, heroism is a necessary condition for it, and also an acid test of non-violence. There is no correlation between non-violence and cowardice. Vardhamana became ***Veera*** [the brave] on the strength of non-violence and he became Mahavira by adopting it his life.

Non-violence has the power, which cannot be conquered by anyone. In the time of Buddha, Angulimal, who wore garland of fingers extracted from the bodies of people killed by him, once faced Buddha. Gautama Buddha was passing on his way when Angulimal came in front of him and he challenged Buddha to change his route, but Buddha did not care for his challenge. He was an apostle of compassion [the ***karuna***] and compassion is the best supplementary value of non-violence. In this way, even being full of compassion, Buddha was definitely brave also. Why should he be afraid of Angulimal? Buddha went on walking and at one time both were in front of each other. Buddha stood before him with strait eyes, but Angulimal could not see eye-to-eye; he got defeated and became Buddha's follower. This was the strength of non-violence.

Many more such examples can be cited, but here I will discuss only one example more, which is related to Mahatma Gandhi and then give full stop to my talk. It was the month of March in the year 1930. Mahatma Gandhi was proceeding towards Dandi from his ***Sabarmati Ashram*** of Ahmedabad. A man of a place near Bharoach, who was opposed to the principle of Gandhi, threatened him to kill in a lonely place. Anyhow, Gandhi got the news. He was a worshipper of non-violence and, therefore, fearless and brave also. He knew that anyone having ill-will cannot withstand before the power of non-violence. Two-three days passed. In the meantime Gandhi got ascertained the name and address of that ill-willing person and one day, in early hours, he confronted him. Gandhi told the man, ***"Brother! I am Gandhi; you want my life. Take it soon, none will know."*** The man could not see eye to eye with the votary of non-violence and became his follower. This is the reality of natural, dynamic and active or live value non-violence and of non-violent hero.

9. Morality: A Fundamental of Civilization Dedicated to Human Welfare

A review of thousands of years of human history, in which various civilizations raised their flags in different parts of the globe, from time to time, confirms the fact that morality always remained established in human society in both forms, direct as well as indirect. Morality, as one of the strong supplementary value of non-violence, not only existed, rather it functioned as a guide remaining active and dynamic in daily chores of man; and ultimately it called for all-round human welfare and inspired man for this purpose.

Since morality remained dedicated to human welfare, and played important role in making and unmaking of various civilizations, it is necessary that we should get introduced to the meaning of morality.

In India, from very ancient times, consistently and under all circumstances, the message was for progress and welfare of all, general and particular; and while doing so, it was declared that ***"this is the highest moral law"*** and if ***"we all adopt this live truth, all laws relating to morality will themselves appear."***

According to ***Bhagvadgita*** morality is a part of duty. But of which duty! Generally of the same duty, under which actions for prosperity of all are accomplished without any self interest, without any desire or expectation of reward and by dedicating to that symbol of oneness, the God. No doubt, this is a repeat of message of human welfare in the ***Gita***.

In Indian philosophy morality has also been treated as dharma. By doing so, it has been said ***"in real terms man can be called moralist, or in other words dharmic [religious], if he is above hate and selfishness, whose life is perfectly pure and who is involved in service of all. Only such a person can best perform for humanity; and truthfulness is the basis of all this best and highest."*** All-important concepts regarding dharma, like "***adoption of goodness or the best***" or "***discharge of ones duty***" are incorporated in this declaration. Not only this, a scholar, while expressing his views regarding relationship of dharma and morality, has even said, ***"If we loose the morality like base in our life, without any doubt we get separated from dharma."*** According to this scholar, ***"There are no religious discourses that are not moral. For example, a person, who talks of torture and repression, and act untruthfully, he cannot claim to be following the path of God."***

Clearly, here the good deeds also become the acid test of morality. Such deeds become worth following for others, besides individual welfare of man.

All principles and practices of Mahatma Gandhi have been full of morality. Let us see what he says about morality. At one place he says, ***"True morality does not lie in following the path of defeating others, rather to search the path of truth for self and in fearlessly following it."***

In this very context, at another place Gandhi says, ***"In fact, the life of a moralist is full of virtues, or in other words, he leads a life full of virtues and that too, not for the reason that by doing so he is benefited, rather because this is the law of his existence; definitely it is the base of breath. In very brief we can say that virtue itself is the reward of man."***

After all here we have discussed about noble deeds; they are made the basis of morality, and it is dedicated to welfare of all. ***Dharma*** [whether adopting goodness or discharging duties or in whatever context] is bound by it and the path of truth passes through the domain of morality. In simplest language, or speaking clearly and also in brief, morality is the best manifestation of true virtues, with which duty is inseparably linked, and saying again, its objective is the welfare of all.

Above described meaning, explanation and objective of morality is not confined only to Indian concept; scholars, philosophers and thinkers from the West, who have spoken or written about morality, more or less, agree to this meaning, explanation and objective. In this context, first of all, let us talk of German scholar G. F. Nikolai. According to him, ***"There is no logical system behind the concept of moral feeling, rather it is natural disposition inherited from [ones] ancestors."*** In the explanation of Nikolai, thus, there are three dimensions about morality:

- It is a naturally developed sentiment;
- It is linked to duty and is a subject of '***action***' not of '***logic***'; and
- It is in competition with immoral deeds.

According to another German scholar Martin Nimular, all, general and particular, should follow the life style and ideals of Jesus Christ and practice them in their life; life and deeds of Christ were the climax of morality. Simultaneously, many other thinkers of the West have, more or less, expressed the same views, and not only in the philosophy of modern thinkers, but they are found in messages of ancient thinkers like Socrates also.

Ultimately, views of both, the West and the East, about morality are almost similar. Both are near to each other. Let us think, if Nikolai treats morality as natural, and by linking it with duties, find it involved in competition with immorality, where does great man like Mahatma Gandhi define it against the concept of morality in ***Srimadbhagvadgita***, or ***Vedas*** ? Side by side, if Martin makes Christ, whose life and deeds were dedicated to welfare of all, as the base of his principle of morality, where is the difference between his concept and the concept of the East, and especially India? Not only this, in my own view, even social thinkers like Bernard, who suggests two separate concepts of morality for man and woman, are not out of the above field.

D

MISCELLANEOUS

1. For the Establishment of a Peaceful World

My native village Kakrauli situated in the Northern India has inhabitants belonging to different castes and creeds. During my childhood I found all the people of my village out to help one another in their difficulties, sorrows and miseries. In welcoming and looking after their guests they had no comparison. Besides, I also saw disputes erupting among them and resultant clashes. There used to be clashes almost daily on one issue or the other. Sometimes a small alteration tended to threaten the peace of the village by taking a communal colour. Many villagers would be injured in the free for all battle that took place and the matter would go to the police, although such a situation arose only rarely. But in most of the cases the warring groups would lose their belligerence overnight. Non-violence would cool down their tempers and consequently both the groups would reach a mutually agreed compromise. This compromise was either brought about by themselves or through the efforts of some respectable inhabitants of the village.

When I grew up, I often heard about brawls and clashes in the neighbouring villages. Whenever these clashes took place between two villages, instead of two groups of a village, the situation often turned serious. I would often be scared of such a development. Then I would hear of an amicable settlement. The five chosen members often brought about the solution from each of the two villages. These persons would sit at a place and go over the whole problem and in due course of time strike a mutually agreed formula. Sometimes their dispute would lead them to the court, as they would hope for a victory in their own way. The case in the court would drag on for days, months and years. Soon they would get tired of this lengthy and exacting process. Then it would force them to enter into a dialogue. Consequently they would agree on a point that the court was not going to be helpful at all, also the fact dawned upon them that the decision of the court could never be in consonance with their wishes and what they had thought would never become possible.

With the passing of time I grew up to achieve adulthood and from radio and newspapers and magazines I came to know that such clashes were frequent in larger towns and cities besides my neighbouring villages and these clashes would often take a serious turn. I also came to know of disputes specially boundary disputes and the disputes on sharing of river waters among different states of the country. But these disputes were quite different from the ones, which arose in the villages or towns. However, solution to all these disputes would be made through negotiations.

Similarly I found nations involved in dispute and wars, which were undoubtedly diabolical and destructive, particularly the one fought between my country and Pakistan in 1971. Not only that I know of such wars fought between many nations and I also remember how these belligerent nations ultimately arrived at a compromise and a treaty after getting tired of violence.

History is a subject of my interest. Thus while browsing through the pages of world history I have gone through the description of many disastrous wars the description of which even today is heart rending and moving. For instance, the Peliponishial fought some 2500 years ago was the fiercest and the biggest war of Greece. It lasted for 27 years. The provocation of this war came from the mutual jealousy and rivalry among the Greek city-states. Similarly, three Punic wars were fought between 264 B.C. and 149 B.C. and similarly two world wars were fought in the 20eth century. I do agree that I am interested in history but I shall avoid touching upon these wars. Let us not fix responsibility for the outbreak of these wars but I would like to bring to light the results of these wars.

The First World War [1914-1919] claimed the lives of as many as 10 million people besides 22.5 million who were either injured or rendered invalid cripples. Most of the countries of the world took more than ten years to stand on their own feet.

In the Second World War [1939-1945] not less than 50 million people were killed besides 35 million who were either badly injured or maimed. It took the belligerent nations more than 15 years to pave the path of development. The warring nations after getting tired of the wars and the naked dance of death aspired for peace and pacific measures. There efforts in this direction resulted in the formation of the League of Nations after the First World War and the U.N.O. after the Second World War.

A number of instances can be quoted from the later period and the Arab – Israel conflict is a recent example. After the termination of the World War II, this conflict continued for a long time and resulted in an irreparable loss. The year 1967 presented a heart-rending and ferocious spectacle. Most inhuman incidents took place causing a big loss to man and material. But both the sides had to, in the long run, adopt pacificator measures and had to sit together for a meaningful dialogue. The war between Iran and Iraq continued for many years. It resulted into the loss of men and material, wealth, and famous industrial towns. A huge quantity of oil-a gift of nature to man was destroyed. And when they were completely exhausted they had to adopt the same policy about which I have talked to you.

The following points emerge from the discussion starting from the disputes at the village level to the wars fought at the international level:

- Disputes, clashes and struggles right from the lowest level up to the highest plane are quite natural in the human society;
- Nothing has been gained from all these disputes and clashes;
- The belligerent parties feel completely exhausted in the long run and then they try to find out peaceful means to solve their disputes; and
- The belligerent nations have no alternative but to fall back upon agreements and treaties.

History provides us instances where we find wars among nations continuing for many years and sometimes even for more than one hundred years. Although on surface all the four points discussed above may not be found working, yet a closer and deeper scrutiny would prove these points fully applicable to them.

It makes amply clear that violence based on disputes, struggles and mutual clashes are not permanent ingredients of human character otherwise he would not get bored and tired of them in the long run and would not try for peaceful solution to his problems. This undoubtedly proves that man is basically non-violent by nature and violence is born out of his actions only. Had violence been an essential instinct of man the whole mankind would by now have been wiped out. It is non-violence which has helped man to grow and keep his existence secure. Mankind can never remain unaffected from strife and struggles, which have multi-reasons to cause them. This is termed as a passing necessity of the society. But we have been taking peaceful measures in order to initiate it as such measures are indispensable for the existence, progress and well being of mankind. They provide protection and security to human existence and then peaceful living is the very essence of human life. Non-violence, as has already been stated, is permanently associated with it. Thus non-violence and peaceful measures are essential and eternal.

Then there is a need for making efforts at the individual and collective levels so that a fearless and peaceful order is established. First step is to work as individual to cultivate a non-violent permanent perception and then to give it a collective shape later on. This is possible because one is closely associated with the other. Thus we can get rid of all tensions, clashes and wars after we realize the importance of non-violence beginning with individual and then growing into a collective, national and international realization. This is a truth and a reality. I have come to realize this fact as an essence of my life. You too will share my belief if you ponder over it.

I would like to return to the point where I started my discussion. At the very outset I had stated that measures taken to resolve disputes emanating among inhabitants of my native village were very simple. First of all the two or more persons or group of persons involved in the dispute would assemble at a place. Some elderly, mature but impartial gentlemen would control the highly agitated persons. The starting of negotiations would help create non-violence impressions in the surcharged atmosphere. After listening to all the concerned parties, the situation was discussed threadbare and a conclusion reached which would be as under:

- The party or person found guilty was asked to express regret which he would willingly do and the dispute or problem was finally resolved;
- The guilty besides expressing regret was asked to compensate for the loss of the aggrieved person or party. The guilty would often accept it which would finish the dispute permanently; and
- If the clash was of a fierce nature, involving grievous injuries, or even death of some person the matter had to be taken to the police. But the above-mentioned processes were certainly followed in such matters as well. The problems were definitely resolved although it took relatively longer time in such matters.

Similarly, I saw disputes between two villages being resolved. Respectable persons of both the hostile villages known as ***Panchas*** [five or more number from each village] would sit at a place and taking on the responsibility would resolve the dispute amicably. They would sometimes give a wonderful evidence of their maturity. Sitting at a common place, they, accepting their lapses and realizing their regrettable stances would bring about a permanent solution of their disputes. However, compensation was also included besides expressing regrets and realizing mistakes in graver situations and everything ended in the permanent solution of the dispute.

Disputes among the states were also resolved through the efforts of ***Panchas*** who held meetings and dialogues for this purpose. However, the process is absolutely different so far as the nations are concerned. There is national and international politics besides the other considerations. But they have to go through the process of a series of meetings and talks to arrive at the final solution. There too non-violence originates from such efforts, which certainly are a step towards establishment of peace. Then start meaningful negotiations keeping in view the larger interest of human beings. There is an evident progress in this process, which ends in inevitable compromises and treaties. Thus the path beginning with negotiations and ending in the solution is paved by non-violence and is ultimately a step towards the establishment of peace, which helps in the solution of all the problems whether big or small.

In order to substantiate my point I would like to quote a statement of Dr. Ezer Weizmen, a renowned fighter pilot of World War II then posted in India and who has been the President of Israel. Mr. Weizmen, through a horrible fighting, had scored a thumping victory over Egypt in 1967 during the hostilities between Egypt and Israel. Later on it was he who played a crucial role in the Camp David Deliberations. In a statement made a few months ago he had stated:

"We have finally decided that we shall have peace with our neighbours. This notion is the result of negotiations and there is nothing on this earth which

cannot be resolved through negotiations". [Times of India, 28.12.96]

He also accepted that there is no alternative to negotiations and had Negotiations with Jordan and Egypt.

The statement of Weizmen is significant and it is a fact as well. Camp David negotiations are well known but I can quote the example of Hebron negotiations. It took a long time to reach a conclusion but it succeeded in the end. The Parliaments of both the countries ratified the decisions and accorded their consent to it. It proves that the people of both countries really wanted it.

In 1996 India and its neighbouring nation Bangladesh concluded an agreement, which was regarding the sharing of waters of the River ***Ganges***. In India had constructed the Farraka Barrage, which was the bone of contention between the two countries. But at last the two countries arrived at a mutually agreed understanding which is welcome.

The ***Panch*** system is not only significant rather it is the best system. It involves meetings, compromises, treaties etc. However, it does not seem to be that much successful at the international level as the role of ***Panchas*** cannot be above Board, though there is nothing wrong with the system as it has recourse to non-violence, which helps establish peace.

Non-violence and the allied tendencies help generate peace, which is indispensable for the existence, progress and growth of human life. As discussed earlier, non-violence is an indivisible part of human nature. Therefore, when we make efforts for material progress at individual, social, national and international level, we should leave no stone unturned to make it strong and all pervasive.

Today, the whole of the world is aware of the fact that nothing can be gained from violence and war. These are not going to solve any problem. Unfortunately no firm and meaningful steps have been taken to eradicate violence and its creations, the war. There is a prime need to root them out. Schools, colleges and universities will have to come to the forefront. I am sure that even if 5% of the revenue spent on progress and development of the countries is directed to it, we shall definitely find a comfortable, beautiful and pleasant world free from war and other allied tensions.

Please ponder over it and work in this direction, I have come here today to give you this message.

2. Problems before Society and Nation and Obligation of Intelligentsia

It is natural that problems crop up in day-to-day human dealings. This is not a matter of worry or anxiety. It is, however, necessary that problems must be solved per apt thought. Apt thought is necessary so as to avoid facing these problems soon again. It is expected in human world from a being. These problems again appear soon when a person solves them while keeping selfishness at top and does not prune them with apt thought. They are more serious when they appear a 2nd time. Resultantly, human life paces towards a difficult future. Others also come under its effect. A thing in relation to an individual is also in relation to a human group. After all, a human - individuals form group. As such, when a human society solves a problem instantly with auto-selfishness without apt thought, the solution badly impacts not only that human-group but whole society and nation: whole human world sometimes. This obstructs the way of development along with disintegrating society and nation.

Such a thing happened with our society and nation also and is still happening. As a result, serious situation has emerged before society and nation. Foremostly, four problems are responsible in this regard. These four are interlinked in absolute manner. They have also accord impact, more or less, on one another. This is like a situation where our body catches one ailment and we do not take a right and comparatively permanent remedy. The ailment appears again after some time and brings with it one, two or even more other diseases. The body fails to fight such a situation and its situation becomes serious. A question crops up pertaining to very existence of life of human concerned. Subsequently, whole human-group gradually comes under grip of the disease. The disease of one person transforms itself into an epidemic and extinguishes many lives. Four main problems are:

- Population;
- Corruption;
- Defective Education System; and
- Caste System

Population of India was 33 ***crores*** when India gained independence. Now it is 100 ***crores***. Such an immense increase in population within 50 years shall certainly create vivid problems at individual, social and national levels. Along with such a huge population, it is difficult to fulfill five fundamental human necessities - food, clothes, housing, education and medical aid. Employment to all is something specifically appreciable. Increasing population shall definitely create serious problems: in whatever quantity natural resources are there in a country. Arab nations have oil storages. They are considered rich in this respect. But amongst them there are many, especially country like Iran, where 18% to 20% people are unemployed. The main reason behind this all is population increase.

Look at the condition of India. Even today, people in many parts of the country are having an income of 100 Rupees per month or below. A lowest level has been prescribed - even if poor .... such an income must invariably be with an individual for subsistence. It is unfortunate that 40% of the people have failed to reach up to this minimum income level in our country. That evidently proves them to be below poverty line. Increasing population is the main reason behind it. Similar conditions prevailed in other countries whenever population increased in this way. In case, we are poised to bring a progress into this nation and wish to take people to a way of life imbibed with pleasant, prosperous and peaceful attributes, we shall have to control population increase of such a dimension.

Second problem is of corruption. Really speaking, it is an international problem. Along with Asia, it is also there in Europe and America. We can peruse and understand this from the grafts, which were sought in preceding years. We have an example of Thailand in the preceding year before us - the Prime Minister Silpa Archa had to vacate his office owing to being fully involved in corruption. Indonesia's condition is no better. But condition of India is somewhat abundantly poor. It is needless to mention as to how much we are in grip of corruption. Probably, there has hardly been any region or person that could not be under its impact directly or indirectly. Rulers, bureaucrats, workers and others: it appears that all are under its grip.

Our whole system is like a body. Vivid nerves in body are full of flows of blood just like actions taking place in vivid parts of any system. Now, it seems as if corruption is rampant in the system, which can be compared to a body, and this is happening practically. Now, this is a subject not only of our concern but that of existence of respectable life. I am not mentioning any individual or institution in particular but you all know that those individuals and institutions, which claim that they are there to take nation towards development and to give clean governance to nation, are actually fully involved in it. There is a question mark on our national character. Certainly, our dignity and honour have been severely tarnished by this.

The third problem is defective educational system. When I use the word ***defective***, it signifies that this education is not complete in imparting self-sufficiency. It is incompetent in getting a graduate obtaining employment and in getting he/she developed. We have been treading on a traditional and rotten way since a very long time. We did not sufficiently ponder over or act in this direction according to time and circumstances. Resultantly, twenty *crore* people of the country are under penance of unemployment. Think for a while the circumstances under which a country shall have to proceed; where people happen to be unemployed in such a huge number.

Along with this, the educational system also seems to be antagonistic to moral knowledge. This is definitely a subject of concern. Moral knowledge is an essential part of education. Education does not fulfill its definition in absence of that; how shall it be able to gain its aim or objective. Good conduct is impossible in absence of knowledge. Resultantly, personal and social life shall become vicious. We have certain expectations from an educated person. In case these are not fulfilled, its straightforward and simple meaning as it appears is that he/she is devoid of moral knowledge. Diminishing moral values and standards are the reasons behind the present situation in public life. Defective education system has been constantly causing vices. This should not continue henceforth.

The fourth and the most fatal problem is caste system. This system has been rooted there for centuries. It is assumed that this system came to be there in place of class system. Why? When? And how? Several expressions have been there on this. I am not mentioning them here. It will not be contextual to do so. Even then, I shall like to remind that it is said about class system [and it is also mentioned here and there in treatises of ***Vedic*** Religious Community] that it was based on labour division system in human society. Its basis was work not birth. Lord Buddha[1] and ***Tirthankara*** Mahavira[2] also supported it on the basis of work. On this accord, even though the topic is interesting, I shall not elaborately explain it here, as it is not my intention to put a thesis or research before you. I may do that separately. I certainly wish to emphasize that we now do not have the class system that was in former times. Now, there is a question relating to caste system that is based on birth in our society. We produce religious arguments also in its favour whereas religion is not at all concerned in relation to caste. Caste has concern with definition or meaning of religion. Ordinarily, religion signifies adoption of goodness.

This is the reason that eternal human values, which guide to welfare, come under purview and embodiment of religion. Non-violence, non-conservation, abstinence from stealing, compassion, sacrifice, justice, truth equality etc., all have been considered religion. Caste system is symbolical of inequality and it divides. It is full of exploitation and selfishness. How can it be termed proper in context of religion?

Number of castes in our society is about 4 thousand. Let us assume that all believe in one God. Every one has even then a separate mode of living. It's very plain meaning is that our society is divided into 4000 parts. This division is symbolical of inequality. It certainly makes the principle of fraternity and spirit of justice insignificant.

We talk of faith in one Almighty. God is the father of all. He is just. There are many other things also that we say about God. We also talk of ***Vasudhaiva Kutumbkama*** [This earth is a family]. But we have been sticking to caste system for centuries whereas this system is prone to signify inequality and injustice. This is our way of thinking and mental application. Let us for a moment analyze it with truthfulness and impartiality. We shall find that this system always disintegrated us. It took our hearts away from each other. It has harmed us. It many a times gives us bondages as per several bad customs and usages. It has even made a deep gap betwixt man and woman. Even today, we can see it on social, political and economic levels.

We may give numerous arguments in favour of this system and we may try to prove it adequate by citing examples from religious treatises. This is against that Divine principle on which we claim that it is practiced by us. It is certainly totally opposite to the principle of equality, fraternity and justice and is full of selfish spirit. It has been showing itself in every age and is still showing.

As such, these four are serious problems before our society and nation. They have gradually developed owing to indifference and apathy to one's duty. More than these, selfish motive is the cause behind them. We are facing them today. In case these problems happen to be there before other societies and nations in addition to India, causes of their existence and development are the same.

It is responsibility of intellectuals in every age in every society and nation that it must accord guidelines towards solving the problems truthfully and impartially. Intellectual class has its own specific position in a society and nation. This class is competent in solving problems constructively. It is our misfortune that intellectual class is not doing this truthfully and impartially. It appears that it is itself under the grip of these tangible problems. Now, what conclusion should be derived? Are intellectuals far from their duties? If it is not so, they will have to accord guidelines with truth and impartiality. It is what society and the nation expect from them. Ultimately, we cannot turn our face from truth for very long. Truth is truth after all. We shall certainly suffer if we disassociate ourselves from that. We are disintegrated; ourselves. We have divided ourselves; in case we want this process to continue, we can gladly choose to keep ourselves away from truth.

References

1. Gautama Buddha stated in ***Dhammapada*** [***Shloka*** 393) ***"Na Jatahi Na Gottehi Na Jacha Hoti Brahmana, Yamhi Sachacacha Dhamma so suchi Sauch Brahmana."*** It means - No one can be ***Brahmin*** as per tress, clan or birth. ***Brahmin*** is one who is incorporated with Truth and Religion: Only then he can be termed as pious. He stated at another place: ***Jacha Na Baslo Hoti Jacha Na Hoti Brahmano, Kammana Baslo Hoti Kammana Hoti Brahmano;*** It means - one can not be ***Brahmin*** by birth and not even Taurus. Man can be ***Brahmin*** and Taurus by deeds only. It indicates that Gautama Buddha was not against prescribing class of a person in accordance with his/her deeds.
2. ***Tirthankara*** Mahavira also stated [***Sutrakritanga*** 9/2] - ***Brahmin, Kshatriya, Vaishya***, they are accustomed to other works. He also said [***Uttaradhyayana*** 25/33], ***"One can be Brahmin, Kshatriya, Vaishya or Shudra on the basis of his actions."*** This also clarifies that he was in favour of class system according to deeds.

3. India and the Asian Values

Existence, progress and ***achievement of goals***, is a sequence on which the values in this world are formed. ***'Non-violence'*** is a permanent feature of human nature in the absence of which very existence of man is not possible and it is the most benevolent, most natural and foremost of all the values. The virtue of ***non-violence*** leads all and because of this, man formed itself into a social group. Till then he had been wandering aimlessly and then he decided to settle down at a place in the company of others. After that began his social life. Thus for the achievement of this settled and social life, non-violence is essential as the existence of mother is essential for the birth of child. Thus the first thing to develop in man was non-violence, which was already ingrained in the nature of man. The very existence of man would certainly have come to a naught in the absence of non-violence. Hence non-violence is the foremost and natural and universal value. It is because of this reason that every prophet or enlightened man has regarded non-violence of paramount importance, but it became the very core of Jainism.

II

Non-violence, the permanent part of human nature was at the root of man's desire for permanent settlement and a

social life. It helped man make his existence safe and sound. But something more was needed to make it enduring and ever-growing and to help take steps on to the path of progress. Thus man in all his settlements took pains to fix certain values of life. Those people along with their progress through over the issue of purpose of life and spared no efforts to empower these values for the achievement of progress and attainment of goals. Although the values come into existence according to the changed circumstances yet their motive continue to be the same and that is – the future of mankind should be safe. It should make endeavours for an all-round progress and try to achieve its ultimate aim. The accepted values are inclusive of all the aspects of life backed by a strong philosophy.

After universal acceptance of the foremost value of non-violence, whatever human values came to be recognized became a beacon light from Asia for the whole of the world. Asia gave birth to ***Vedic*** philosophy, Jainism, Zoroastrianism, Taoism, Confucianism, Judaism, Buddhism, Sikhism, Christianity, Islam and Wahabites and they are flowered and developed in this continent. Each of them showed its followers the path of righteousness. They showed them the right path of life, besides calling upon them to embrace some particular values and ideologies in the practical life. It can be safely stated that the ***Vedic*** philosophy emphasized forbearance and tolerance; Jainism, non-violence; Zoroastrianism, unity; Taoism, humility; Confucianism, equality; Judaism justice; Buddhism, compassion; Christianity, service; Islam, brotherhood; Sikhism, bravery and Wahabites, harmony to be adopted in the philosophy and conduct of life.

India holds a unique place so far as the position of Indians in Asian values is concerned. ***Vedic***, Jain, Boddh and Sikh values were born in India and they flowered and prospered in this country. These values instructed man as to how to lead a purposeful life and how to progress towards his ultimate aim. There is no doubt about the fact that the values established in other parts of Asia were influenced by them. Later on they spread all over the world. However, it would be proper to dwell upon the chief Asian values before we discuss the Indian values and ideologies any more.

III

I have already stated that these values got established in different parts of Asia according to change of time and conditions. Who so ever enunciated them, whether a learned man or a scholar or a prophet, these values were supported by some philosophy or the other. It would not be improper to discuss the philosophies or the religious communities associated with these human values.

Vedic: The ***Vedic*** values, philosophy and the associated religious community are respectively known as Hindu values, Hindu philosophy or the Hindu religious community. ***Vedic*** philosophy and the ***Vedic*** values are quite ancient. Many saints, scholars and prophets were involved in the establishment and the process of growth of these values. Their most significant and chief notion is that God is Supreme and Man is the noblest of all the creatures. Action or ***'Karma'*** and ***'Jnana'*** or ***'knowledge has the utmost importance in human life.'*** It is the duty of man to progress on all the fronts and to seek salvation is this ultimate aim, which leads to the supreme peace.

As I have already mentioned, non-violence is natural and universal. It has a very important place in ***Vedic*** values. Forbearance and tolerance head all the teachings, which the ***Vedic*** values impart to man in his daily interactions. Besides this, good conduct, morality, compassion, duty and faith are among the significant human values. The ***Vedic*** philosophy established these human values so as to discipline man.

Jainism: Jain values and philosophy are rather ancient. Twenty-four ***Tirthankaras,*** of which the first is Rishabhdev and the last Lord Mahavira [599-527 B.C.], shaped the philosophy and considered ***'non-violence***' the basic value of man to be the foremost among all the human values. All the principles and codes of conduct are guided by it. Jainism considered non-violence to be the be-all and end-all of all human activities. It instructed everybody to be non-violent in words and actions and also to follow truthfulness, non-indulgence in theft; ***'Brahmcharya'***, and ***'Aparigraha'*** in order to maintain compassion and friendship.

The Jain values and philosophy have been present in India since the times of ***Vedic*** values and philosophy and even before that. ***Non-violence*** indeed leads all those virtues as its ulterior motive is to live, progress and to achieve the aim of life it salvation and also it calls upon the others to live, let live and to achieve the ulterior motive. It has the capacity to win for man the ultimate aim of salvation through the trinity[1] of faith, thought and conduct.

Zoroastrianism: Zoroastrian values and philosophy was originated in Iran during 2000-2500 B.C. Zoroaster was the propounder of this philosophy. His message was that God[2] is one. All the creatures are born of Him and are thus equal. Declaring ***unity*** to be its mainstay Zoroaster wanted to probe deeply the ***truth*** and also called upon the people to put it into actual practice. Besides he wanted the adoption of generosity, brotherhood and equality. His fundamental views were that enemy could be won over into friendship and even a stupid and unwise person could be changed into a wise person. Such were the values of Zoroastrianism by which mankind could be united into a single whole.

Taoism: The values and philosophy of Taoism originated and developed in China during the reign of Chou[3] dynasty keeping the contemporary social conditions in view. Taoism called upon the people for the adoption of virtues like kindness, selflessness, introspection and accumulation of knowledge and spirit of sacrifice. He called upon the people to lead a life embracing all the virtues.

Confucianism: Confucius propounded his philosophy in China [551 B.C. – 479 B.C.] at a time when morality and humanism had reached the lowest ebb there. Keeping ***equality*** as a paramount virtue, he opposed the practice of slavery tooth and nail as it amounted to exploitation of a human being by his brethren, in the presence of which progress of man was impossible. How could there be morality and good conduct in the society when a feeling of high and low prevailed among the human beings. Confucius, therefore, declared equality as the characteristic of man and said:

"Don't treat others in the manner in which you don't want yourself to be treated."

Thus these are the essentials of humanism and morality. In order to establish equality between man and man he wanted the adoption of morality and good conduct, which are the pillars of humanity, and for that purpose he recommended the adoption of seven virtues in one's daily conduct.[1] These virtues are:

- ***E*-duty;**
- ***Chui*-beneficence;**
- ***Chun*-faith;**
- ***Bhu*-forgiveness;**
- ***Vain*-human love;**
- ***Sin*-honesty; and**
- ***Siao*-humanity**

Confucius laid emphasis on religion, politics and the unity of the society for achieving equality among human beings and declared morality to be at the very basis of all conduct. He considered the present life of man to be of great importance and said:

"Must do one's duty..."

For this purpose he called upon people to adopt the following five principles in their life:

- Rulers should respect their subordinates;
- Parents should be kind to their children who on their part should respect their parents;
- Husband should follow a good moral conduct and the wife should obey her husband;
- Elder brother and sister should realize their duties and the younger should respect and obey them; and
- Friends should have a mutual trust.

Judaism: Moses advocated dignity and respect for all the human beings at a time when injustice prevailed and even brothers turned into enemies discarding distinction between good and bad, forgetting the Almighty God. This was a real path of truth. He called upon people to follow the tenets of compassion, humility, courtesy and love. He wanted all the human beings to adopt transparency and purity in their relations at all levels be they the members of a family or a society. Thus this is the very basis of the philosophy of Moses and its scope is not limited but all pervasive.

Buddhism: Lord Buddha [557-477 B.C.] establishing compassion as the basic value wanted man to realize his central position. He discussed in detail the causes of human misery and the ways and means to resolve them. He gave message of compassion besides noble deeds, sacrifice and truthfulness in day-to-day human conduct for the realization of the ultimate goal of salvation. He called upon people to adopt the middle path.

The Buddha invoked people to adopt rectitude in relations at all levels. He also laid emphasis on introspection.

Sintoism: Sintoism originated in Japan. Love is at the basis of this philosophy, which draws its potential from the following five basic values:

- Love for God [as according to Japanese opinion, they, their forefathers and emperors were born of God];
- Love for nature [as nature is the dwelling place of god];
- Love for cleanliness [as god loves it];
- Love for fortitude; and
- Love for ease but while doing noble deeds [because it is a gateway to success].

God [of which everything is born], nature, cleanliness, fortitude and ease are essential aspects of human life. It is on the basis of these that man should conduct his daily life. And it only can lead a man to his ultimate goal.

Christianity: While acquainting the sinful mankind of the knowledge of ultimate truth Jesus Christ endeavoured to establish Christian values and as it has already been said ***service*** topped the Christian values. Besides it called upon its followers to adopt the values of compassion, love, good and noble conduct in their lives. He considered sins to be at the root of degradation of man and called upon him to commit himself to God the Almighty. If somebody is hungry, a Christian should offer him food. If the food he has is just sufficient for him then he should share it with the hungry. It is always better to offer than to accept.

Christianity urges requital of love for enimity. Peace lies in the service of others. Refraining from murdering someone, corruption, theft, false evidence and having good relations with the neighbour and carrying out all duties are among other virtues of Christianity.

Islam: Brotherhood is the top most of the values of Islam propounded by Prophet Mohammed. It is against the principles of humanity to have enimity among brothers and human beings. All men are the creation of God, the Almighty. Therefore, they should profess love for one another by remaining bound together with the ties of brotherhood. Besides they should adopt forgiveness, justice and good conduct in their actions. They should refrain from addiction, usury and corruption. The respectable should be shown proper respect and those who deserve love must be loved. The Prophet urged his followers to adopt three main principles in their daily conduct. They are:

- To speak humbly;
- To offer ***Namaz***; and
- To give ***Zakat.***

All three go a long way to bring glorious future to man besides making his conduct better and ensuring him the achievement of ultimate aim of his life.

Sikhism: The main values of Sikhism, which came into its full flowering by the contribution of its ten Gurus are:

"Praise Him as God is one and the father of every creature. He is omnipresent. Man should earn his livelihood truthfully and honestly and should share his food with all."

Sikhism believes in one God and gives the message of equality by considering all the human beings as His creation. It has been strongly affirmed:

"God created all the human beings through His light. No one is good or bad having been born of that Celestial light"

Sikh Gurus fought against various ills prevailing in the society of their times. Many of them even sacrificed themselves in order to protect mankind. This sacrifice signifies their bravery. Therefore, bravery is the hallmark of Sikhism. The followers of Sikhism even go to the extent of sacrificing their lives to protect women, the helpless and the weak.

Wahabites: God is one and He is the fountainhead of all the religious philosophies. He reflects Himself in everybody. Therefore there cannot be any distinction between human beings. We may differentiate between human beings on the basis of caste, colour or birth, but these classifications are not justified. Such are the ideologies by Wahabites. When there is no difference in human beings, all are equal and have the same origin then why not establish harmony among them. Now the main point is as to what steps should be taken to consolidate this harmony. Values of this community affirm that everybody should get equal opportunities. Love and compassion should prevail, distinction between poor and rich must go and women should be equal and truth should be universal. Good conduct should be a part of daily human conduct. People should adopt justice and humility in their actions. Wahabites also urge the adoption of love for action, good living, self-dependence and refrain from the consumption of alcohol.

These are some of the chief Asian values. Some common points of these values are:

- The Supreme power is God whom people call by different names. God is the father of all creatures. He is the fountain head of all powers and worthy of worship;
- Man is supreme among all creatures. He has a purpose life and it is his duty to achieve it;
- Action is the most important part of human life, because on action depends every result;
- All creatures – men and women are equal. They have equal rights and responsibilities; and
- Daily human conduct should be based on excellent ideologies, which should be based on truth and purity.

IV

India enjoys a unique position in Asian ideologies. The life of Indians has been guided by ***Vedic*** philosophy for thousands of years. Although the philosophy and values of the pre-***Vedic*** period lie beyond the scope of the subject-matter of this paper and it would be out of context to dwell upon them and moreover no historical record of that period is available, yet I can safely affirm that these values were definitely influenced by the ***Vedic*** values and philosophy.

We can easily perceive that influence in the day-to-day human conduct especially in the context of livelihood, methods of worship and family atmosphere.

The values and ideologies came into existence as a result of meditation and contemplation and accumulation of knowledge by several philosophers, saints and sages. There is a definite contribution of those great men who showed path to men from time to time. Such ideologies and values are so that man should not forget his duty towards his creator, as He is the Truth and a source of peace and is justice incarnate. Thus man was to keep constantly in his mind the presence of his creator and whatever action he performs, he should keep His presence in mind.

This entirely means that action is of utmost significance in human life. On human deeds depends the existence, progress and aim of his life. He can perform his deeds independently but the fruit of his deeds depends upon the kind of deeds he has performed. In case he wants progress and the achievement of his goal, he will perform the deeds, which are most virtuous, and the noblest. Man has been blessed with intelligence and he is the Supreme creature. He can differentiate between good and bad, between truth and falsehood. ***Vedic*** values expect him to conduct himself reasonably well in his routine behaviour.

Jain values have existed in India even before ***Vedic*** philosophy and values came to India. Keeping non-violence at the centre of all thoughts, Jain values placed before man the integrated form of meditation, speech and conduct. They endeavoured to bring human life in a strict discipline. They also maintained strict values of food. They declared knowledge of the Self, essential for progress and realization of the Self and declared salvation to be the final goal.

Jain values laid stress on ***Karma*** to be of utmost significance for man. Growth and decline are the result of one's ***karma***, although Jainism, unlike ***Vedic*** philosophy, doesn't believe in the omnipotence of God. Jainism expects a man to perform ***Karma*** on the basis of his judicious reasoning.

Values are always maintained for the over all benefit of man. It creates a problem when a man or a group of men become indifferent to the realities behind the values and use them for the fulfillment of their selfish motives. This is what happened when the Buddha was born. The followers of ***Vedic*** values had got busy in the fulfillment of their selfish motives. They had started declaring God, the Almighty, as their personal property. A particular group of persons had started using religious scriptures as their own property or the property of their own group. In such circumstances Buddhism with the middle path at the centre of which was compassion, influenced the whole of India. Later on it influenced the life of inhabitants of different parts of Asia. Several Buddhist values got influenced by the ***Vedic*** values. It was a similar case as that of the ***Vedic*** values being influenced by the ***Dravidic*** values. Undoubtedly the Buddha did not accept the existence of God, in the way the ***Vedic*** ideologies did. He even challenged the ***Vedic*** line of thinking about God. But his views about compassion and amity, the importance of ***Karma*** the result according to one's actions and the philosophy of rebirth, were influenced by ***Vedic*** values. Guru Nanak who was born in Punjab a state of India founded the Sikh values some 500 years ago. Many Sikh values like Supremacy of God, the importance of ***Karma*** and the belief in re-birth carried the ***Vedic*** influence. Guru Nanak himself like Lord Buddha and Lord Mahavira was born in a family, which believed in ***Vedic*** values. Guru Nanak refused to accept any distinction between one man and the other on any basis. He laid greater emphasis on devotion than on knowledge. He condemned bigotry. The later Gurus slowly learned towards the idea of bravery and thus bravery took the supreme position in Sikh ideology.

Thus all these four values – ***Vedic,*** Jainism, Buddhism and Sikhism – were born or bloomed and grew in India. Zoroastrians came to India some 1300 years ago and settled permanently here. The Islamic values came to India some eight to nine hundred years ago. All these were not born in India but they continued to stay here along with others, which had already prospered here. These values certainly influenced the prevalent values and in turn left their influence on them as well. It can very easily be perceived in daily conduct, food habits, dresses, way of living and other social activities.

We are well aware that at first ***Vedic*** and later Buddhist values spread from India to other countries of Asia. The neighbouring countries did come under the influence of ***Vedic*** values although Buddhism spread quite far and wide. China is a neighbouring country of India and both the countries have very close social and cultural relations spreading over thousands of years. Both Taoism and Confucianism were born and blossomed in this country. Buddhism spread to China from India and the Chinese values influenced Indians particularly those living in the northeastern region of this country.

Buddhism reached Japan as well and it influenced the life of the Japanese. Hence all the values where ever they were propagated came under the influence of India and in turn influenced the people of India as well. Thus India is a place of fusion of all the Asian values. All the values became a part of the life of Indians. In India we can find the very essence of all the ideologies for leading a virtuous life. We can still find in India the ***Vedic*** and pre-***Vedic*** family systems. We can still perceive here tolerance and other ***Vedic*** values which help achieve an all round progress and the ultimate aim of life. All these ***Vedic*** values, which help us, realize our duties and modes of conduct are still prevalent in India. Non-violence of Jainism and compassion of Buddhism and other values still continue to be an essential part of the Indian way of living. Similarly protection of the helpless, food for the hungry and prayer to the almighty form a vital part of our conduct which has been re-established in the shape of the values of Sikhism.

In India can be found service the most significant of the teachings of Christianity along with ***human-unity*** of Zoroastrianism. Here can be found the principles, morality, righteousness and justice besides the values of brotherhood. As already stated, we have in our country an influence of all the Asian values and followers of different religious communities living here adhere to their discipline. ***Vedic*** values do not direct the life and conduct of the Hindus only. They influence the life style of all the inhabitants of this country whether they are Christians, Jains, Parsis, Buddhists, Muslims or Sikhs. Similarly other values, whether they were born in India or whether they traveled into India from other countries, influenced the life of the Hindus. I am of a strong opinion that all the Asian values can be found in harmony with each other in India. They shall continue to remain intact in India till the existence of India as a nation.

References

1. Rishabhdev is the first Jain ***Tirthankara*** whereas Lord Mahavira is the last and there are twenty-two ***Tirthankaras*** between them.

These ***Tirthankaras*** are – Ajitnath, Sambhavanath, Abhinandannath, Sumatinath, Padamprabhu, Suparshvanath, Chandraprabhu, Pushpadanta, Shitalnath, Shreyansnath, Vasupuyjya, Vimalnath, Anantnath, Dharmanath, Shantinath, Kunthunath, Arhanath, Mallinath, Suvratanath, Naminath, Neminath and Parshvanath.

2. In Jain philosophy they have been mentioned as three gems [***Triratnas***].
3. In Zoroastrianism God has been addressed as ***Ahura Majda***.
4. 1122 B.C. – 156 B.C.
5. Confucianism used ***LI*** and ***ZEN*** for morality and humanity respectively.
6. The Buddha emphasized eight truths [eight fold path], which help root out human miseries. Main among them are: Right word, Right action, Right effort, Right thinking, Right living and Right concentration.
7. Salvation and detachment.
8. Sintoism advocates cleanliness of mind. The cleanliness of mind can be classified into [a] white pearl like cleanliness of mind; [b] cleanliness with the brightness of sunshine; [c] Cleanliness of mind for justice; and [d] Cleanliness of action depending on noble deeds.
9. The propounder of Sikhism is Guru Nanak Dev, other nine Gurus are: Angaddev, Amar Dass, Ram Dass, Arjundev, Hargobind, Harrai, Harkishan, Teg Bahadur and Gobind Singh.
10. ***Vedic*** or Hindu values are a part of Sikhism.
11. Here I am referring to the ***Dravidian*** values in which agriculture and animal husbandry being the chief profession, gregariousness of human nature from the point of view of security, love for peace and a good neighbourliness are some of the most prominent values. We find them in the ***Vedic*** philosophy as well. This is the reason why I have emphasized that ***Vedic*** values carried the influence of the former values. This is quite natural. After all these values have come to stay for the welfare of mankind as a

whole. Thus how can one overlook the old values while establishing the new ones? That is why ***Dravidian*** values of the former times helped in the establishment of ***Vedic*** values.

12. It appears that the Jain values existed even before the ***Vedic*** values and during the ***Dravidian*** period. At the time of creation of ***Rig-Veda***, these values were there in the shape ***Muni***. In this regard we can quote ***Rig-Veda*** [10/136/1] to prove our point. The word ***Aharat*** as used in ***Rig-Veda*** is also the meaning of the word ***Jain*** as used today.
13. The Buddha adopted all the ***Vedic*** values, which appeared to him to be most practical. But he called upon his followers to eschew those, which did not appear to be practical and useful.

4. Nuclear-Religious Conflicts and Peace in South Asia

I am myself a citizen of the South Asian Country India, the country that always accorded message of peace to world. It gave birth to eminent apostles of peace like Lord Buddha, Lord Mahavira, Guru Nanak and Mahatma Gandhi. You know that India is the biggest and a very important nation of South Asia. It is also the biggest democracy of the world. Most of what is known as South Asia today was formerly India. Burma was part of it up to 1937. Today's Pakistan and Bangladesh were its part up to 1947. Nepal and Bhutan have remained connected with it. Not only this, several parts of today's Central and South East Asia have been in India. As such, India cannot be separated from any event in South Asia – the event may be big or small. In case of a question pertaining to peace in this region, it can be safely stated that it is also impossible without India.

As I have enunciated, India always kept the flag of peace high what so ever circumstances, internal or external, may have been before it. It is an irony, however, that such an India, its neighbour Pakistan and nearby Sri Lanka are under a state of turmoil today. Other nations of the region are also under turmoil. Conflicts between religious communities and sects are the main amongst the responsible factors. The nuclear tests undertaken by some countries recently have enhanced this turmoil. This is a reality.

Development of any sort, individual, social, national or global, is not possible under a state of turmoil. You as well as I can well understand the situation that will emerge under non-development. It is on this accord that constant end of turmoil and establishment of peace are essential attributes. To achieve this goal, it is necessary for us to remedy the state that has emerged out of turmoil caused by religious conflicts and the nuclear tests. The question arises as to how to achieve this goal. To get a reply we shall have to go into realities of both the religious and the nuclear conflicts and to maximum possible extent peruse their historical perspectives, especially the religious conflicts, that too severally.

Religious Conflicts, Historical Perspective and Impact

In spite of indispensably being connected with religious assumptions and rituals, if we delve into ancient history of Southern Asia, we come to know about conflicts between religious communities and the followers. Under this chain, we can foremostly mention about conflicts between ***Aryans*** and ***Dravidians*** however we do not have a clear history pertaining to that. It is however certain that after the conflicts, the religious assumptions and rituals became assimilated[1]. Subsequently, the ***Vedic*** system known as Hinduism today became life ground of most of the Indians. I never say that there was not a conflict between those who belonged to ***Vedic*** system. There emerged vivid sects in this system and there were conflicts also within these sets. Even when non-violence is permanently present in human nature, time-to-time, there emerges a state of conflicts in practice even if the related practices are religious. Such a state of conflicts actually emerged. However, internally no serious situation emerged owing to the conflicts between the religious sects. India could continue sending message of peace to world.

In Buddhist-Era[2] there were many followers[3] of Jainism[4]. There were six sects[5] under operation in ***Vedic*** community. All among ***Vedic*** were the believers in ***Vedas,*** and ***Brahmins*** enjoyed supreme position/status in them. Buddhism and Jainism-both-refused their faith in the ***Vedas*** and challenged the ***Brahmins*** enjoying super status in the system. Although they did not accept the concept of GOD, even though, they accepted many other virtues[6], specifically Lord Buddha from ***Vedic*** system and ideology.

Lord Buddha opposed all inhuman actions that were prevalent in ***Vedic*** philosophy, system and community with an aim of peace because up to now different sects of ***Vedic*** religious community were not proving peace-oriented to common man even though they were uniform regarding ***Rule of Almighty*** and *State of* ***Vedas*** *and* ***Brahmins.*** The fact was that in practice they departed from ***forbearance***, which is the principal Value of ***Vedic*** system and ideology, and Lord Buddha was accordingly in action as above. Lord Buddha established a ***middle path*** towards a system where man could safeguard his existence and could gain aim of life with equality and honour. He accorded ***compassion*** as the position of basis of his philosophy. It was essential in the circumstances in accordance with the time and factors belonging to the country. India and nearby regions became followers of Buddhism in maximum number. Subsequently, Buddhism dominated Sri Lanka and other nations.

I hold Jainism to be quite ancient to ***Vedic*** one. Jain philosophy was present among ***Dravids*** prior to the advent of ***Aryans***. So to say, a section of ***Dravids*** adopted Jainism. It could have got a new direction during the time of Lord Mahavira. Non-violence, permanently present in human nature, is the basis of this philosophy or religious community. This is the way towards peace.

In this manner, in about 500 B.C., three foremost religious communities – ***Vedic*** [Today's Hindu], *Boddh* and Jain had followers in Indian region [Today's Pakistan, Bangladesh, Burma etc. along with Afghanistan, Nepal and Bhutan]. These three had sects and there were conflicts as well, specifically in ***Vedic*** community. Even after that, a serious situation, such as in the last era[7] of Mughal dominance, as we find in history before us, did not take place. The time of British Empire[8] and independent India[9] can also be equalled with the last era of Mughal dominance in this regard. The reason behind this had been that there had never been intrinsic fundamentalism in ***Vedic*** religious community. The practices of the followers became opposite to real values. In spite of this fact, it can be stated that forbearance and tolerance continued to be present. A place for internal criticism was there.

Gautama Buddha himself was born in a ***Vedic*** family. He criticized many practices and dogmas of ***Vedic*** system and established ***Boddh Religious Community***. Lord Mahavira was also from a royal family. He too refused Vedic rules like Lord Buddha and, as we know, he occupied position of 24th ***Tirthankara*** of Jain religious community. Not only this, members of two different sects of ***Vedic*** Community could be a person of the same family. If husband was a follower of ***Sanatana*** sect and wife of ***Arya Samaj*** the two could easily live in a single home by following their respective rules.

Of course the ***Vedic*** people deviated themselves from basic assumptions of religious community to fulfill their individual and collective ends. This was the very cause of conflicts internally. We can apply this cause towards conflicts of ***Vedic*** community with other communities. But, I again firmly reiterate that this conflict is not at all in consonance with dictums or lessons of any religious community. Every religious community was established with many values in accordance with circumstances pertaining to the country and time. However, one among these values has been principal and the aim of establishment was to ensure that a human being should have development and achieve peace while carrying out daily practices.

When conflicts were there in sects and communities, social, political and economic spheres were impacted. Culture was hurt and resultantly miseries and grievances had to be faced. This happens to be a reality. After Lord Buddha, there was no serious conflict in religious communities or sects and to this what so ever reason we may attribute. If we study present history, which is before us, and if it is true, we see that during the last phase of Mughal empire[10], situation became serious owing to fundamentalism. Not only Hindu religious community but other communities and sects also became victim of this fundamentalism. Resultantly, there were conflicts as per opposition. These were specifically from Hindus and another newly established community, Sikh, amongst Hindus. We all know that this religious stiffness, even though far away from the teachings of Islam and Prophet or the lessons accorded by them, is one of the main factors that caused disaster unto empire.[11]

It is a fact that differences enhanced among vivid religious communities at this time, however, it is also a reality that the people of India [mostly rural inhabitants] grasped Indian traditions. Hindus, Muslims, Sikhs and all others lived together and continued practices according to their beliefs. It is, however, a reality that there were persons who used to cause disharmony in society on the pretext of community or sect.

The Englishmen had an ambition to strengthen their hold pertaining to governance of the country and so they adopted a policy of ***divide and rule***. They not only materialized direct conflict betwixt Hindus and Muslims but also adopted such administrative cum political measures, which could deepen communal difference between the two. Division of India in 1947 on the basis of religious community resulted owing to this. Historians are aware that first of all Hindu-Muslim conflict occurred in 1893 in Mumbai and after that in ensuing year 1894 at Pune and the imperialistic government had its hand in these conflicts. Subsequently, hundreds of conflicts ensued. The Englishmen could not stay in India in spite of treating on the above-mentioned policy.

India became independent in 1947 and was partitioned into two. A nation named Pakistan emerged along with India. As this nation came into existence on the basis of a specific religious community, the people were exchanged from India to Pakistan and vice-versa. This was unfortunate. The two should have treaded the path of development in spite of all this. This did not occur. Development was there but peace could not be established. Communal conflicts caused harm unto each of the two severely. The arms race betwixt the two in parallel dimension shattered external peace. Now the situation is that in India there have been about 5000 communal riots between 1947 and 1997. These riots were mainly betwixt Hindus and Muslims.

Definitely thousands of people lost their lives in these riots and property of crores of rupees was destroyed. In Pakistan also there have been conflicts between sects or amongst members of one particular sect and also between two communities. The number of such riots happens to be in thousands. Loss of lives and property in Pakistan has been as serious as that in India. Other nations of South Asia are also not peaceful.

In case the nations of South Asia want prosperity, development and ultimately peace, they will undoubtedly have to establish harmony amongst different communities and sects. Without harmony we cannot imagine peace in this region. For this ambition, it is necessary to attempt at three levels:

- State or government;
- Community; and
- Individual

Nuclear Tests and Impact on Peace

I have clearly stated that some nations of South Asia advertently conducted nuclear tests recently in the garb of security and this has resulted in enhancement of non-peace in the region. In case we really wish to go into depth of these tests, we will have to deeply examine and study the series of events on the world after the World War Second generally and in Asia, specifically. Many of you are familiar with this series of events. Today, there are about 3500 atomic warheads in the world. Maximum attack capability of an atomic bomb serves as safety measure from attack capability of atomic bomb as the whole world becomes under this attack capability circle.

In this situation, I have no reason to hold that any one from the nations with atomic capability shall be courageous enough to initiate atomic war. I do not perceive that India shall be attacking Pakistan with atomic weapons or that Pakistan will be taking such an initiative.

Reality remains that atomic conflict or tension thereto is not a problem that is confined to South Asia. It has increased non-peace in the whole world. All nations with atomic capability must, now, march forward seriously pondering over the destruction of atomic weapons and to utilize this capability for the cause of humanity. They should come out of the atmosphere of fear and must march forward towards peace. It is only fear that is stimulating nations to get themselves equipped with atomic weapons and accordingly to make them. If the trend of making atomic weapons continues, the fear will be increasing at its more rapid magnitude. This fear will one day bring humanity to disaster and doom.

I would like to urge here that those who are playing political game and fulfilling selfish motive in the name of atomic capability need to think on all this. Is it nice to conduct activities at the cost of whole humanity on this accord? An action that is suicidal is indeed deplorable. Manufacturing atomic weapons is really a dangerous game.

We were deliberating on India and Pakistan. India is the birthplace of too many apostles of peace and it happens to be the biggest nation in South Asia. It is my firm conviction that there cannot be any problem, which can resist a solution per peaceful means. These are the means, which were adopted by apostles of peace. Any problem or dispute, how so ever big or small in magnitude, can be definitely solved by mutual understanding and purity of heart.

It is in this regard that I hold that being free from all disputes; India will have to render leadership to world towards getting the world free from nuclear weapons. There is no other alternative. Pakistan should imitate India subsequently. India and Pakistan are neighbours. Both these nations are facing common problems and hurdles. Why not these two should work for pleasantness, prosperity and peace through grasping responsibilities unto them? Why not these two should comprehend reality of international politics? They must fully utilize their capabilities in the direction of solving day-to-day problems of their citizens.

Not only in India or Pakistan, in other nations also of South Asia, 30 to 50% population happens to be below poverty line. It signifies that the people below poverty line have no guarantee of even two-times meals. They do not possess clothes: even though they are quite essential. There exists no apt arrangement for their houses. They are far from the facilities of education and medical treatment. How can we think about peace in such a situation? We can make progress in field of science and technology, we can gain atomic capability but we must understand that we cannot claim any development without fulfillment of basic human necessities. All nations of South Asia, including India, shall not only have to ponder over it; they will have to absolutely conduct themselves in this direction.

I reiterate that none of the nations, that possess atomic capability, are courageous enough to initiate a war with nuclear weapons. It is because every one very well knows the consequences. Even if some one dares think ahead in this respect or line of action, I guess that it will itself back out. There will not be a repetition of those things which occurred at ***Hiroshima*** and ***Nagasaki*** on August 6 and 8, 1945.[12] Whatever occurred there was the first act of this kind and I think that it will remain to be the last act.

Now, when India and Pakistan have gained atomic capability, they must fully utilize it towards nice pursuits. All nations of South Asia, including India, are quite lacking in comparison to America and Western countries in the field of grain-production. Other agriculture-products are also comparably far from satisfactory. This capability can be well utilized in the field of agriculture-produce. This will accord us freedom from the problem of food. Those who are still in want of food, the basic need, shall get welfare unto them. Nuclear capability can be utilized in the field of transport as well along with a progress in the span of agriculture. This will ensure progress in the field in addition to ensuring freedom from the problem of pollution.

India and other nations of South Asia have a dearth of electricity. Every body in countries of South Asia today is not getting benefit of the electric-power. Nuclear capability can bring, never-before, reforms in the field of electricity. It can increase production to such an extent that every person can derive benefit out of it. Why is this capability remaining non-utilized to its full extent? Nuclear capability can be utilized for health services as well. We can utilize it towards a relief from diseases of serious nature. We are facing a dearth of fuel for cooking. Atomic capability can fully bring an end to this problem on earth. Every household can benefit out of it.

Apart from above there are many other fields in which nuclear capability can prove to be a boon. It can be an assisting factor towards upgrading the standard of living of common man. India will have to march forward in this very direction and field. Pakistan also has no alternative except to follow. It is also expected from other nations of the region.

In this manner, on one side the nations of South Asia, especially India and Pakistan, will have to establish cordiality betwixt different religious communities and followers of various sects and on the other, they will have to strive hard to desist from all pursuits relating to armament-including the desire to go ahead in the field of nuclear weaponry. The capabilities achieved in fields of science, technology and atomic energy shall have to be well utilized towards making life of common man happy. This is not only my expectation; it is as well the responsibility of both the nations. The two cannot be indifferent or escaping in relation to this responsibility.

I have already stated that there is no problem that cannot be solved by mutual rationalization and through peaceful means. The dispute relating to Kashmir is a very small problem from this point of view. There must be purity of heart. This dispute can be solved in a short time. I am myself keen to suggest a solution if it is accepted with truthfulness. This problem should certainly be accorded a solution positively now. Subsequently, peace should be established through intrinsic cordiality and external friendliness and the whole region must pace forward in this direction.

References

1. ***Aryans*** came to India about 2000 B.C. At that time, ***Dravids*** were the inhabitant of India and they had their own religious

assumptions. Peace happened to be the supreme amongst them and it was based on ***Collectivity in life*** followed by non-violence. ***Dravids*** were peaceful but they were not uniform in respect of religious assumption. I mean to say that there was no uniform religious assumption in the whole Indian region [India, Pakistan, Bangladesh, Burma, Afghanistan etc.] Uniformity began to emerge here after the advent of Aryans: whatever the means might be.

2. Between 563-483 B.C.
3. Amongst main followers: Veerangak, Veeryash, Sanjay, Eneyak, Say, Shik, Udayan, Shankha, Kashivardhan. Additionally, Dashambhadra and Chetaka were there.
4. Lord Mahavira, the 24th ***Tirthankara***, was present at that time and many had become his followers along with those belonging to royal families.
5. ***Vaisheshik, Nyaya, Samkhya, Yoga, Meemansa*** and ***Vedanta.***
6. Virtues like non-violence, stiffness, sacrifice, tolerance and forbearance. Lord Buddha transformed these into practice.
7. 17-18th Century A.D.
8. 18-20th Century A.D.
9. Time up to now since 1947.
10. Specifically in period of Aurangzeb.
11. Mughal Empire.
12. Atom Bombs were dropped over two cities of Japan – ***Hiroshima*** and ***Nagasaki*** on August 6 and 8, 1945. Approximately one hundred thousand people instantly died and if we count the number of persons dead consequent to the impact of these bombs, it comes to about 350 thousand. The persons, who died subsequently, were victims of diseases viz. intrinsic bleeding, leukemia, cancer and such others – the diseases that spread owing to the impact of these bombs. Many ensuing generations had to be under above-mentioned inhuman deed informing of victims. Many infants were mentally and physically handicapped at birth itself. Many had to face difficulties relating to health. Temperature of the places, where bombs were dropped, stayed betwixt 3000

and 4000 degree Celsius. Only 1550 degree Celsius is required to liquidize iron. Many people perished under severe heat of these bombs beneath the process of liquidization. Their eyes were found burst-out and in this manner they became victims of an act which was inhumanitarian in toto.

5. Indian View of Peace

India, the land of ancient culture and civilization, holds a comprehensive, extraordinary and unique place in context to peace. Thousands of years ago the message of peace conveyed by this country had a deep impact on the entire world. The main reason behind this influence is that approach towards peace that has directly or indirectly been built by contribution of knowledge obtained and deed and of course real experience. It may be clarified by the following ***shloka*** from an old Indian treatise in which Nachiketa[1] says:

"Shanta Samkalpa Sumana Yathasyad
Veetmanyugaritmo Madabhimratyon,
Twatprasrishtam Madbhivadeta Prateeta
Etattrayanam Prathaman Vara Vrane"[2]

That means:

"Hey Mratyon! May father Gautama [Vajashravas] of mine be peace tempered gleeful, anger less and have peaceful thoughts towards me as before? May he talk to me, after identifying my deputation by you? This is the first boon that I demand out of three boons accorded by you."

The above-mentioned ***Shloka*** relates to a mythological tale. May be this tale does not interest you. I myself don't deem it necessary to present it here. But the heartfelt feeling, which is at the root of the ***Shloka***, definitely reflects the outlook of India towards peace from times immemorial.

Just as evident in the ***Shloka***, Nachiketa was promised to ask for three boons. In first boon he desired his father to be peace tempered, gleeful, anger less and have peaceful thoughts towards him i.e., he personally expected this. Just as this clarifies the Indian view of peace from ancient times, it also clarifies that the Indian approach towards peace starts at personal level. Therefore it becomes collective, social and later moves on to national level. An important reason for this is that Indian philosophy depicts that human being is either rewarded or punished according to his deeds. This is something extraordinary from the peace point of view, and it is so because the efforts made by individuals for establishment of peace are of utmost importance. In other words individual efforts work as foundation stone in constructing a building of peace. We all know that a society or a nation is built when men get together. Thus the rise and fall of a society or a nation depends on them.

The above ***Shloka*** from ***Kathopnishad*** is just an example. The ***Vedas*** were in existence hundreds of years before ***Kathopnishad*** was composed. And even in the ***Vedas*** we clearly find a clear view pertaining to peace. ***Vedic*** prayer ***Shanti Prakarana*** can especially be quoted by us in this regard. Not only this, even prior to ***Vedas*** we came across peace related concept in day-to-day behaviour of Indians more or less. And similarly the same can be observed from past to present times. Before and further discussion on the subject, it would be better for us to know about the meaning of peace and its purpose in brief.

Generally, peace is termed as a condition that is opposite to conflict, struggle that peace is an atmosphere devoid of conflict, struggle, war or violence as a scholar says: ***"It is symbolic of an atmosphere free from conflict, struggle..."***

In the same way another scholar believes: ***"Peace is, generally, negatively conceived as absence of war and struggle. In other words, peace means absence of actual violence."***

All this, even then, does not express the complete meaning of peace. This is true that there is absence of conflict, struggle, war or violence in state of peace but it is not limited by this alone. The scope of peace is vast and in my opinion it only ends when a human being attains the aim of life.

For peace whatever else is required, other than end of conflict, struggle, war or violence, is related to day-to-day practices of man where co-operation and harmony is essential, that too from inner core of heart, so that even in general state man's heart is at peace and he may realize peace in thoughts and deeds. And that harmony may be such as has been expressed in form of expectation in this ***Shloka*** of ***Atharvaveda***:

"May we be in harmony with our kinfolk, in harmony with strangers, do ye, O Ashvina! Establish here agreement among us;

May we agree in mind and thought, may we not struggle with one another, in a spirit displeasing to the gods;

May the arrow not fly when the day of Indra has arrived."[3]

I mean to say that meaning of peace; in general conditions[4] is fulfilled only when it exists in man's heart, in his daily practices or actions and thoughts. This is what really stands for. In this way peace is neither the subject of any particular time nor is it negative value.[5] This is, in itself, a positive and an active value. In the words of Vinoba Bhave:

"By peace or Shanti... do not mean something static or the perpetuation of the status quo. Shanti means something dynamic, something that develops the force of the individual, which develops the dynamic strength of the people to a degree that will enable to meet any situation."[6]

Mahatma Gandhi, accepting it as positive, connects it with morality and ethics and proclaims that the impulse behind ***shanti*** is a desire for spiritual contentment, an impulse free from ***Kama*** and ***Ahamkara*** [the desire for enjoyment and egoism]. That is why he has laid emphasis on realization of the feeling of brotherhood and has desired that a man should identify himself not only with other men but also with all existing life on earth and this identification is the symbol of harmony.

II

Just we have discussed, that in all branches of Indian philosophy,[7] it is proclaimed that ***man*** is the centre of the deeds and on the basis of the same he gets results whether good or bad. He is superior among all living beings and occupies the most important place. It is expected from man that keeping his existence safe he should proceed towards all round development. It is also expected from him that he should attain the real aim of his life.[8] How should he do this?

The propounders of Indian philosophy have guided him from time to time in this regard. On the basis of their experience that they gained through knowledge and deeds, according to the circumstances pertaining to their country and times, they exhorted man to follow those values that can create best, congenial and harmonious atmosphere for him. All these values are supplementary to non-violence.

Whether it is forbearance or tolerance, the principal value of ***Vedic*** [***Hindu***] philosophy or the ***Karuna*** [compassion], a value established by Gautama, the Buddha, all have been supplementary to non-violence and in this way they all proved to be the best, effective and strong bases for harmony. And why would it not be so? After all the aim of all philosophies is peace.

Today when we talk about world peace, we feel that it will not be possible unless each and everyone gets equal opportunity for his/her progress or unless everyone is sure of fulfillment of his/her basic needs. Peace is not possible unless everyone has the liberty of self-expression, or it is just a dream if each and everyone is not accorded freedom, justice and rights. I would like to clarify that all above mentioned values, supplementary to non-violence, were established for the reason that everyone could easily be brought under the circumference of equality, freedom, justice and rights, including the right of self expression, i.e. without exercising any force or without using any violence.

Not only this, goodness like equal respect for everyone's faith, complete absence of fundamentalism, unity of mankind etc. were propounded by the leading figures of the society through above values. From time to time they also shared their experiences with people so that they may be inspired by it. These values are as important today as they were in the past or during the time of their establishment. Even today if we inculcate these values in our lives, according to our circumstances and need, we can create a good atmosphere of harmony and also march forward in the direction of peace.

In fact, thousands of years ago, Indians had firmly experienced that non-violence, as an immortal value-permanently present in human nature, is not only essential condition for existence but also for the development and to reach the real goal-peace. That is why the propounders made relentless efforts to base the day-to-day activities of people upon non-violence and its supplementary values. In this task they not only achieved expected success but they were able to set such examples, knowledge of which surprises us even today. It is because in those days the means of transport and communication very limited and underdeveloped. But they were able to comrnunicate the message of ***ahimsa*** in a simple way, along with Indians, to inhabitants of different parts of the world. But, as has been stated, they did so by creating a conducive atmosphere as per the demand of times and country's circumferences. In this regard we can do so then definitely many volumes can be written. That is why here I shall only quote two great men of ages.

In the times of Mahatma Buddha the state of Indian society had seriously and greatly deteriorated. People had started going against the values established for the safety of existence and progress; they were getting avert to non-violence and its activities. Besides inequality there was exploitation, so much so that there was inexpressible extreme of it in human acts. At such a time Gautama Buddha propagated the value of ***Karuna*** that is compassion, keeping in view the circumstances and need of the time. He set examples for all people, big and small by his own behaviour in life and on the basis of the same, was able to launch an effective and strong movement to reform the society.

From the point of view of that time, compassion was the best expression of non-violence, a good means of establishing peace. As a result after individual awakening, people of India could march in the right direction collectively. It was due to above movement that polluted religious, political and economic sphere also advanced towards righteous goal in a proper way. Later the message of compassion crossed the territorial limits of India and it was able to show the path of peace to other countries of the world.

The other example in the previous century, i.e., 20eth century, is of Mahatma Gandhi. He from his gained knowledge and from the experiences of first half of his life came to the conclusion that Indian people, tolerating the curse of dependence and injustice, can achieve freedom over the mighty imperialism of the world through the means of non-violence, and can perpetuate the path of peace for itself, and also can show a unique and significant way to the whole of the world. He lead the Indians for about 25 years i.e., from 1917 to 1942 through various non-violent ***Satyagrahas***; worked to wake up their slumbering consciousness, infused a new life into them and ultimately in 1947 India became free from British Imperialism. This was not an ordinary event in world history. But all this became possible because he developed the concept of non-violence according to the conditions and needs of his life. [9]

He astonished the world by making experiments through non-violence at different occasions, with a firm belief that ahimsa is the oldest, greatest, and perpetual and an active value connected integrally with truth. After that people from a number of countries could learn a lesson by his unique non-violent way. His path proved to be a source of liberation for them. In this context we can quote the ***Afro-American Campaigns for Civil Rights*** of 1955, 1961, 1963 and 1964. Not only this, we can also mention here about ***EDSA Revolution in Philippines*** in the year 1986 in this context.

Some people are of the opinion that the view of non-violence in context to peace is not very effective. In this regard they also quote the examples of Buddha and Gandhi. But such people should remember that neither the concept of non-violence of Buddha nor of Gandhi, or generally of India, is that to surrender before injustice or to become coward. One who is a coward, or one who bows before injustice, can never be a possessor of ***ahimsa***. Along with Buddha and Gandhi, generally Indian view of non-violence is to establish its concordance with prevalent circumstances and needs. Even then it is certain that non-violence is the only pathway to peace. This is the experience of India.

In today's scenario or series of events at national-international level, sometimes it seems that what non-violence would do? How peace will be restored by non-violent means? In this regard I would again clarify that to bow before injustice of unjust, to tolerate tyranny of tyrannous is not the outlook of Indian non-violence. After all how can be peace established in a state of injustice and tyranny? Of course, Indian view is to fight against injustice and atrocities through non-violent means as far as they are possible because there is no other alternative to them. In the words of Lord Krishna:

"Even if any non-violent way is available, we should give up violence and adopt the non-violent way."[10]

If this is not possible if there is no hope, let this be eradicated by least possible violent means and thus peace be established. And even while doing so the inner feeling should be non-violent. We should not have ill feelings towards unjust and tyrannous. Indian non-violence is complete in its meaning and aim when it remains in our heart, words and deeds. This indeed is India's viewpoint. Also this is its experience of non-violence.

References

1. A character.
2. ***Kathopnishad.***
3. ***Atharvaveda***, 7:52:1:2.
4. Free from conflict, struggle, war or violence.
5. Manu, the Father of ***Vedic*** Laws, and Kautilya, a renowned statesman of ancient India, consider peace to be the subjects of a particular time and declare it to be negative value. About the state of peace it has been mentioned in the ***Manusmriti*** that when king knows that at some future time his superiority is certain and that at the time present he will suffer little injury then let him have recourse to peaceful measures i.e. ***YADAVAGACHCHEDAYATYAMADHIKREYA DHIRUVAMATMANAH, TADATVE CHALPIKAM PIDA YADA SAMDHIM SAMASHREYET.*** In the ***Arthashastra*** [1:263], Kautilya has mentioned: ***Who ever is inferior to others shall make peace with him, who ever is superior in power shall wage war-VIGRAHA; who ever thinks, "No enemy can hurt me, nor am I strong enough to destroy my enemy,' shall observe neutrality, whoever is possessed of necessary means shall march against his enemy, who ever is devoid of necessary strength to defend himself shall seek the protection of another, whoever thinks that help is necessary to work out an end shall make peace with one and wage war with another.***

6. The voice of ***Ahimsa***, Volume-VI, Number: 8, August 1956, pp. 279-80.
7. Indian philosophy does not refer to only ***Vedic*** or Hindu philosophy. It includes Jainism, Buddhism and all those philosophies that developed in India.
8. ***Moksha, Mukti, Vimukti, Nirwana*** or ***Parmashanti***.
9. Theory and Practice of Gandhian Non-Violence.
10. Essays on Religion, p. 37.

6. Reverence For All Life: A Move Towards Cosmic Consciousness

It has been depicted, most beautifully and clearly, in the first line of a ***Shloka*** of ***Jinavangmaya*** that ***'SAVVESI JIVIAM PIYAM***, i.e., life is dear to all.' Every living being, to a very intense and significant extent, has the will to live. This is a desire which manifest itself. A living being wishes to live so long as he can. Any person, sentenced to capital punishment if asked suddenly to choose one betwixt whole earth and life, he will choose life. When it is established that all living beings want to live and no one has accorded us a right to kill, there should not be any attempt to kill any one. No one should be tormented. In case we cause to pain to some one, try to strike and injure or try to take some one's life, some or the other will also try to take revenge upon us. This is the very stage to start animosity and hostility. Hence, it is incumbent upon us that we respect the right of lives of all.

The second line of this ***Shloka*** states ***'PANINCHA PIYA DAYA,*** i.e., all living beings cherish mercy' in the same direction as they dislike attack on life. Suppose there are two people standing at a place before an animal. One of them holds a knife in his hand and the other a bunch of grass. Seeing both, even an animal's eyes make it clear that the man with grass in hand is only acceptable to it. So, to give protection to all living beings should be an attitude of man. It should be remembered that one who protects others and has the tendency of ***daya***, he himself becomes fearless. Thereafter he has generally no fear from any person. As such protection is the most important aspect of life. So it has been very rightly said that among all the charities, protection to life is the best.

The third line has the reference that ***'ATMAVAT SARVABHUTESHU,*** i.e., always keeping in mind ***AHO ATMAN*** meaning thereby, to consider all living beings as ones' own self.' To have a feeling of pain/sorrow for all beings of the world, keeping in mind that the affliction is being caused to us, the pain will be suffered by us as by others. While doing so, the last line of the ***Shloka*** directs, ***'RARASPAROPGRIGO JIVANAN'*** which means a person should contribute good will and co-operation to a great extent. The creativity of the creature consists in the fact that he mutually co-operates. It is the only condition to make life worth-living.

At the root of all the above four lines lies complete non-violence which gives the great message of harmony in the best possible manner, keeping regard for all lives. This, in fact, is the only welfaristic way for ones own self and equally for others. The concept of reverence for all lives is evergreen and relevant because only through it anyone and everyone, keeping their lives safe and protected, can proceed towards the goal. Come! Let us continuously advance in this direction.

7. India and the World: With Special Reference to 21st Century

In 1995, the then Ambassador of the Republic of Poland in India, Prof. M. K. Bryski, delivered a Memorial Lecture at the City of Meerut. Prof. Bryski explained Indo-European relations and mainly discussed the role and contribution of India in 21st Century. Not only as an Indian, but also as a citizen of the world, I listened to his views. Many truths about India which cannot be denied by anyone - general or particular - had been touched by Prof. Bryski, therefore, today, I too would like to express my views under the title: ***'India and the world: With special reference to 21st Century'*** in the same manner as done by Prof. Bryski.

In fact India is a mini world. It possesses a civilization and culture, which is thousands of years old. From very ancient times, it has been a spiritual teacher of the World. Many apostles of peace like Lord Mahavira, Lord Gautama Buddha, Guru Nanak Dev and Mahatma Gandhi have taken birth on this land. No other country in the world has probably influenced, in all most all the important areas in the world, as India has done.

Historical evidences have been collected which prove that human life started only from our land. Perhaps, it may be unknown to the present generation that our country has given the best system of governance to the world, i.e., democratic system of governance thousand years ago, and today after completing 56 years of independence, India has set an example of the biggest democracy of the world. This is amazing because about one thousand million people live in India. The citizens belong to different religious communities of the world. In India, there is great variation in the language spoken from north to south and east to west. People eat different kinds of foods, wear different kinds of dress and follow different living habits.

In India the building of social structure is based on thousands of customs and traditions. Indian society is divided between 3500-4000 castes and sub castes. After having such great variations, our country is an example of unity in diversity, and as I have already said, that it is a mini world. It conveys a message to the world and that is:

"Live and Let Live, Progress and Let Progress, Proceed towards the goal and Let others Proceed."

What is the goal? Definitely, to bring peace to the world.

Now these are the days of globalization and liberalization. The world has shrunk; the developments that have never been before in the field of transportation, communication and science have brought people close to each other. Not only this, if any particular event takes place in any country or region of the world and it does not have impact on the other nations of the world, it is not possible, and then India, which is growing as a super power and leading in information technology, biotechnology, nuclear development and space science etc., cannot remain untouched of any event of the world in any condition.

As I have already mentioned, India is a country of unity in diversity. It is the second most populated country after China. It is the biggest democracy of the world. It is natural if its society of diversities faces some problems, if it faces different challenges - internal and external. And it is a reality. I do not deny it.

Internally population causes a serious problem for India, and this problem results in unemployment. Near about two hundred million people, more or less, are subdued by unemployment. Like other nations of the world, corruption sets a serious challenge for India. Poverty is also another serious problem because even today 26 per cent people live below the poverty line. There are also other internal problems similar to those of other nations of the World.

But in comparison to problems and challenges, India's achievements during the past half-century are so much high that other nations of the world, particularly developing and under-developed, can learn a lot from her. Let us discuss India's main and exemplary achievements briefly.

In 1947 India became free from the British imperialism. At that time its population was near about three hundred millions but the food-grains here were not sufficient so that every person could have two meals a day. We were just dependent on other nations for our food grains. Today the situation has changed. The population is near about one thousand million, although this is not the matter of any appreciation but today the food grains produced here are much more than our basic needs. According to a government data, two hundred million ton food-grains are produced every year. After meeting the home consumption, the food-grains are exported to 30 countries of the World. Besides this, there is a heavy demand for Indian tea, sugar along with eatable items and readymade garments in other parts of the world. India is providing clothes to millions of people of more than 50 nations.

About 10 years ago, I was the Vice Chancellor of Meerut University. At that time there were 218 universities all over the country. Now this number has increased to 250. At present all twenty-five provinces of the country have their own universities or equivalent institutions [at least one] for higher education. Most of the universities and their affiliated postgraduate colleges are imparting education full of modern facilities. They also have computer technology and modern equipments. That is why I had already said in the beginning that India is going to lead in the field of science, technology, biotechnology and space science. A country like China is also far behind India in information technology. The United States of America is looking for assistance from Indian engineers to stabilize its electricity supply system. Many Indian scientists have also proved their superiority in various branches of science and technology in different nations of Europe and America. India, as we have heard recently is going to send her scientists on the moon by 2008 and on Mars soon after it for explorations.

According to the figures of the year 2001 near about thirty five million homes were facilitated with cable connection, which, now in my opinion, has doubled up. Near about twenty million people possess mobile phones. All the remote areas have been connected with telephones. India stands in the queue of developed nations in the field of telecommunication.

In today's age of world level competition, capital investment of more than two thousand million Dollars is being made every year. By the end of this financial year, India has a reserve of foreign exchange more than 8, 50,000 million dollars. Every year near about six hundred thousand cars of different models are manufactured in the country. In this direction India is ahead of more than 100 nations of the world.

On the basis of above-mentioned achievements it can be concluded easily that India is not a weak nation. This is a country of high potential and occupies an important position in the world. Her importance cannot be ignored at all in world's development. Along with this her role for the establishment of peace cannot be denied. The world can learn a lesson from her diverse society, and the problems, which are being faced by her as challenges. Significantly, as India has strong moral values, her cultural heritage is alive, there is a commitment of her people towards non-violence - the supreme human value, it is exemplary and to be followed by all in the World.

India faces many external problems. She is bearing the stroke of terrorism for the last twenty-five years. A major portion of the annual budget is spent in Jammu and Kashmir alone to tackle the problem of terrorism. Since India is a secular republic, therefore, some nations try to disturb her secular structure. Why? I don't want to discuss this matter at this place. But sometimes my country faces serious challenges from outside in this context.

India has dispute with Pakistan. Mainly Kashmir is the focus of controversy. She also has some border problems with China. I want to make it clear that India has always been in favour of practicing ***Panchsheel*** principle. She believes in the policy of peaceful co-existence. As I have already mentioned in my speech at the Legislative premises of China in 2001, the whole world has to understand the Indian view of peace. From Indian view point there is no place for weakness. Lord Gautama Buddha, Mahatma Gandhi, Lord Mahavira, Guru Nanak, Vishnu Gupta Chanakya, Pt. Nehru and Sardar Vallabhbhai Patel have played a vital role in her making.

There is no problem-internal or external - at any level of the world that cannot be solved with inter-dialogue or mutual discussion. For centuries this has been the concept of India, which is based on truth. Whether it is China or Pakistan or any other country, all problems can be solved with inter dialogue. Apart from this there is no other more effective or best way in my opinion. Yes two things are important in this regard:

- To be serious; and
- To be ready for sacrifice by accepting reality.

I understand that on the basis of above-mentioned two facts; India will come forward for the solution of her problems. Other parties will also understand the importance of India and will come forward to give the place, which she deserves. India has always been ready for strength and effectiveness of all leading organizations of the world whether it is the ***ASEAN***, the ***SARC***, the Commonwealth or the ***U. N. O.*** especially; India has never turned back in any effort made by the ***U. N. O.*** for creating peace or any step taken by it in this regard.

But, unfortunately India's importance and her role in world's affairs has been undervalued. What is the reason that such a spiritual teacher and largest democracy of the world does not possess a permanent seat with a Power of ***VETO*** in ***U. N. O***'s Security Council? Why is it so that the national language of India, which, is spoken by more than six hundred million people, has not been accepted in the ***U. N. O.***?

Now, the whole world has to understand India's reality. Without this nation's support, progress in any sphere whether it is social, cultural, political or economic would just be a fallacy. All in the world have to construe that India should be given its due place. Each and everyone should take this seriously now in 21st Century. Specially, the people who want peace in the world, they would not stay turned away from India because India is capable of taking the flag of peace and to lead the world in this regard. She has the potential of providing leadership to this world for this purpose. Moreover, it is India's commitment to the whole world, as we can clearly find it in the following words of article 51 of its Constitution that is related to promotion of international peace and security:

"The state shall endeavour to: [a] promote international peace and security; [b] maintain just and honourable relations between nations; [c] foster respect for international law and treaty obligations in the dealings of organized people with one another; and [d] encourage settlement of international disputes by arbitration."

8. Sore Need of Attitude Adjustment

After coming across the three surprising and painful statements issued in these days by the official news agencies and the foreign affairs department of the People's Republic of China, I was astonished. In the first statement issued in Beijing, it has been said that the recent meetings of the 14th Dalai Lama Tenzin Gyatso with newly elected Indian Prime Minister, Man Mohan Singh, and the Chairperson of the ruling United Progressive Alliance, Sonia Gandhi, has not gone well with the People's Republic of China. The People's Republic of China takes these meetings with the Dalai Lama as the Indian interference in its internal affairs. That is why commenting on it, Zhang Qiyue, the Spokesperson of the ministry of external affairs of the People's Republic of China has said, "***We hope that Indian side will abide by the political commitment, refrain from interfering in China's internal affairs and affect the good momentum of Sino-Indian relations.***"

Further she has said, "***The Dalai Lama is simply not a religious figure rather a political exile engaged in spilittist activities... So, the Government of the People's Republic of China is opposed to any meeting with the Dalai Lama by officials of any country in any name or any form.***"

In the second statement issued at Lhasa- the capital of Tibet itself, the Western countries in general and the US in particular has been advised by the People's Republic of China to stay out of the Tibetan affairs. Blaming the Western countries of using the Tibet-Issue as a card, it has also been asked them to leave the Tibetans alone on their own fate.

In the third statement it has been said that the People's Republic of China is soon going to conduct military exercises on such a large scale, that it has never before, to warn Taiwan. But, in fact, I could not understand what is new in the warning to be given to Taiwan by the People's Republic of China which could be considered a different one among the warnings it gave to Taiwan time to time during the last fifty-five years. Rather it would create an atmosphere of confusion fear and instability in the region.

II

The serious political, religious and cultural crises in Tibet, which in terms of race, culture, language, dress and customs has its distinct identity, and which, according to archaeological findings, has its own civilization back to four thousands years, started in the beginning of the 5th decade of 20^{eth} Century with the establishment of Communist regime in the Mainland China that is, now, known as the People's Republic of China. Tibetans, who are religious and peace-loving, had to migrate in huge number from their beloved motherland mostly to their neighbouring country India due to the above serious crises. After that, their supreme religious leader, the Dalai Lama, too, had to take asylum in India in March 1959. Whole world very- well knows this story.

Out of total 1, 11, 170 Tibetan refugees living in several parts of the world viz. Nepal, Bhutan, Switzerland, other Europe nations, Scandinavia, Canada, Japan, Taiwan,

Australia and New Zealand, more than 85,000 are in India. For decades many of them are living in refugee camps in cities like Kolkata, Delhi, Darjeeling and several other parts of the country. It is but natural that several among such a huge number of refugees face numerous social problems there. Also, many among them are affected by the problems related to illiteracy and unemployment. Hundreds and thousands of them are without work. Simultaneously, some times they have to face problems created at the local level. After all they are refugees. Since their supreme leader, the Dalai Lama is very much there, what is wrong in it if he meets Indian Prime Minister or other officials to draw their attention to the problems of his fellow countrymen, or if he urge them to provide assistance to Tibetans on humanitarian grounds? I have no reason to understand that a condition imposed by the side of the People's Republic of China that any meeting of the Dalai Lama with the Indian leaders will irk it, is logical.

Secondly, many a times, reports pertaining to violation of human rights in Tibet have broken the hearts of many, all over the world. Not only the media from the world over, but the report of the United Nations (18/2000) itself has expressed its serious concern over the human rights violation in Tibet. As per the reports available, the number of monks expelled from Tibet, in the past few years, is more than eleven thousands. The persons arrested are six hundred fifteen including one hundred fifty six women. Many among prisoners have died due to inhumanly torture during their imprisonment.

The Culture of Tibet, which has certain religious values in its roots, is, too, facing serious crises. Today, in a population of 2.7 million people, the number of Lamas [monks] is left with forty-six thousands only including

Bhikshunies (nuns). Earlier, they used to be more than one hundred thousand when; forty years ago its population was one million. It is also a matter of serious concern.

In these circumstances too, if the Dalai Lama, from the point of view of justice and freedom for Tibetans, which are the two pillars of humanity, appreciated universally and importance of which has always been felt by mankind, meets other leaders of the world, it is not unjust, improper or inappropriate. However, neither the Tibetan Issue should be used as a card, nor the political use of it should be allowed.

Also, the Dalai Lama has the right to raise the question related to human rights of his fellow countrymen, during his meeting with world leaders, if they are violated, as per the provision of the Article 1 of the UN Universal Declaration on Human Rights (December 4, 1986) which accords:

"The right to development is an inalienable human right by virtue of which every human person and all peoples are entitled to participate in, contribute to, and enjoy economic, social, cultural and political development, in which all human rights and fundamental freedoms can be fully realized. The human right to development also implies the full realization of the right of peoples to self-determination, which includes the exercise of their inalienable right to full sovereignty over all their natural wealth and resources."

After all the People's Republic of China itself is an important member of the United Nations. It is its duty to honour and respect each and every declaration of the United Nation, including that of the Universal Declaration on Human Rights. For this reason, and also to express its commitment towards the aim and objectives behind the establishment of the United Nation, the People's Republic of China should pay attention to the call of the Dalai Lama and the Tibetans. Side by side, if the Dalai Lama draws attention of the Indian officials to miseries and difficulties being faced by Tibetans in India, it is not wise on the part of the People's Republic of China if it treats it as a bone of contention in the process of improvement of relations with India; the People's Republic of China should not take it as an interference in its domestic affairs.

III

Taiwan has made some wonderful achievements in economic and cultural fields and also in technology. A number of goods which comes from its small scale industries have no parallel throughout the world. That is why, today, Taiwan has emerged as one of the economic tigers of Asia. Hardworking Taiwanese, through a well-planned manner, have raised a strong infrastructure. Besides, Taiwanese have given a new dimension to its culture, based on their old but evergreen socio-religious values. It is a small territory but in this manner it has proved to be a country of unity in diversity and diversity in unity. The achievement gained by Taiwanese in both-economic and cultural- spheres are praiseworthy, commendable and every one in Asia must proud of them.

It is a fact the progress been made by Taiwanese in the field of technology has made Taiwan strong. This has given a new turn to the relations of Taiwan with other nations of the world whether they are developed or developing. It is but natural. Also Taiwan has taken certain concrete steps to make it strong from defence point of view. But, the development in Taiwan has presented any serious challenge before the People's Republic of China, or the measures taken about its defence have affected the military strategy of the Mainland, it does not seem to be so. That is why; I have mentioned in the beginning that I do not understand the appropriateness of the new warning of the People's Republic of China to Taiwan.

As far as the question of ups and downs in relations betwixt the People's Republic of China and Taiwan is concerned, they may be tried to normalize in an atmosphere of trust. A process to this effect can be started any time, at any place. I have always emphasized on resolving problems, of any nature or any level, by mutual conversation and compromise. There is no such problem in the world that cannot be resolved through dialogue or discussion. But, as mentioned, it is necessary to create a conducive atmosphere, full of trust, to start a fruitful dialogue. Regarding improvement of relations betwixt the People's Republic of China and Taiwan, the economic and cultural co-operation betwixt the two could be the first and the best step. After that they may enter into other fields and build up a state of co-operation to the extent suitable and acceptable to both.

The People's Republic of China is a powerful country. For centuries it has been said that a powerful country, sometimes, becomes indifferent to the peaceful measures even when there is an opportunity to resolve disputes or problems through them. A powerful country goes its own way. It tries to settle affairs with others through its power. However, the circumstances of the world have changed now. Toady it is not very easy for someone to handle others through its own way. Secondly today no one in the world, who has constructive approach and right thinking, supports the use of power. Also, through power demonstration or through the use of violent means no healthy solution can be feasible. This has to be realized by every one in the world before indulging into any action to be taken through violent means.

9. Taiwan: A Model Territory in the Asia-Pacific Region

With a population of 23.8 million and an area of 35,981 square kilometres, Taiwan is the model territory of people belonging to various religious communities, including Confucianism, Taoism, Buddhism, Yi Guan Dao, Christianity and Islam. This is the territory, which for the last fifty-five years has maintained its unique identity in the Asia-Pacific Region, on the basis of equality and harmony.

In Taiwan, people have staunch faith in democratic system of governance. Although, out of its total population, seventy-six percent of the people speak Taiwanese language but Taiwan is also a nurturer of international languages like English, and several other local languages. About ninety-six percent of the Taiwanese are literate who have been drawing the attention of the world by continuous efforts in raising their standards of living.

As the continuous rise in the standards of living of Taiwanese is mainly due to economic development, therefore, it would be contextual if we discuss here in brief the two major sectors – Agriculture and Industries, of Taiwan.

Like other Asian nations, agriculture is one of the principle professions of the people of Taiwan. About seven and a half percent of the population is directly involved in this sector. Rice is the major crop, which is grown in an area of 332,000 hectares and constitutes to a total production of 1.7 million tons. After this the second in number are the vegetables. These are produced in an area of 174,000 hectares with an annual production of 3,046,000 metric tons. Although more than one hundred kinds of vegetables are grown in Taiwan, but the main among them are bamboo shots, watermelons, vegetable soybeans, cabbages, garlic, cantaloupes, tomatoes, cauliflowers and beans.

In spite of tough competition at global level, sugarcane is also grown in about 32,000 hectares of land. The sugar for the local consumption in Taiwan is mainly sourced from this production.

The production of fruits in Taiwan is good. About 222,000 hectares of land is being used for the production of 2.57 metric tons of thirty different kinds of fruits including, apples, pears, bananas, mangoes, papayas, persimmons, loquats, guavas and wall apples.

II

Fishing and aquaculture is the major industry of Taiwan. In the whole of Taiwan, about 128,000 fisherman households are involved in this industry. About forty- two percent of them are indulged in costal fishing; twenty-six percent in inland aquaculture and the rest are involved in offshore fishing. About 27,500 ships are used to carry the production of 1.32 million tons of fishing products. The total income from this industry is approximately US$ 2.75 billion per annum.

According to my information the aquaculture production, that was about 313,000 metric tons two years ago, has, now, increased by five percent. Livestock industry has grown up to US$ 3.3 million business. This constitutes to thirty percent of the total agricultural production value of Taiwan.

By maintaining eight percent annual growth rate, the manner and the task in which the people of Taiwan have achieved great heights in the economic field through the above- mentioned two major sectors – Agriculture and Industry- are worth adopting and to be followed in the Asia-Pacific Region. It is through this progress that the problem of unemployment has also been successfully dealt with to a great extent. Not only (has) this but because of its economic development, Taiwan has been able to be a part of the World Trade Organization. Simultaneously, it has been able to secure its place in the world economy. Even in the atmosphere of regional tension, it has also been able to influence the Mainland China which can be judged by the information provided to me by a Chinese friend, who has mentioned, "***The business sector of Taiwan has an investment of 32 - 35 billion US$ in the Mainland China.***"

It is clear that in the economic field, Taiwan has emerged strongly and it holds a special place in the newly developing world economy. Being the centre of attraction in the Asia-Pacific Region, no one, including the Mainland could ignore the economic achievements of Taiwan. However, moving on the path of development, many among Taiwanese get doubtful, anxious and fearful of their future. The stand taken by the mighty Mainland China is the reason of that. The reality is also that this situation makes the whole Asia-

Pacific Region anxious as far as the question of stability, peace and development in the region is concerned.

Doubtfulness, anxiety and fearfulness are the biggest hurdles on the pathway of development. It is often that these elements are also troublesome for their origin source. The situation has changed world over now. This is the time for accommodation, interdependence and mutual co-operation. As such the liberal and wise Chinese rulers should think about Taiwan on the basis of goodwill and harmony. Harmony and goodwill are two such elements, which can ease any solution. The present President of Taiwan, Mr. Chen too, has admitted the same view. On the other hand, stubbornness and an intention of using power cannot accord any last-long solution; it cannot make friendly relations and cannot gather any cooperation. This is the eternal rule, an ultimate reality. Experiencing this reality, the dictator like Adolf Hitler after occupying Poland, in 1943, admitted, "One cannot rule by force alone. Even in the land of other's some one needs the local support." Therefore, in the present situation, we should expect a positive approach from the People's Republic of China on the question of Taiwan. Such an approach would also be beneficial not only for China but for the rest of the Asia-Pacific Region. This would also be essential for the People's Republic of China to maintain its credibility and reputation in international affairs.

10. Unproductive Results Without Trust

Even after taking a few steps which can be considered to be liberal in the process of improvement of relations betwixt India and the PRC, the denial by the authorities of the People's Republic of China to Indian engineers expressing desire to visit the site in Tibet where a deep artificial lake was created by a landslide on the river Pareechu and which made the situation dangerous on the border areas of Himachal Pradesh [India] in August 2004, indicated deeply rooted mistrust in their hearts. Simultaneously, after accepting Sikkim as an integral part of India during Indian Prime Minister Atal Behari Vajpayee's Beijing visit in 2002, showing again this territory of Sikkim as a separate nation in the maps by two magazines published in the first week of September 2004 in the People's Republic of China further proved above mistrust. It was also symbolical of frustration and an act of breaking word by the Chinese. In such a situation, i.e., Chinese frustration and a policy of breaking word and double standard, how would it be possible for Indians or others, whether they are Taiwanese or Tibetans, or Mongolians, to improve relations with that country? It is a question answer to which has to be found by the people in the Power in People's Republic of China itself rather than others

It was in mid August 2004 when areas from Mandi, Kullu, Shimla, Kinnaur and Bilaspur districts in Himachal Pradesh were put on high alert following a warning that overflowing water from the above artificial lake in Tibet threatened flash-floods. Due to heavy rain, the lake was brimming continuously. So, it made the Indian side worried. Resultantly, engineers from the Geological Survey of India repeatedly requested the authorities of the People's Republic of China to allow them to inspect the site to extend their co-operation to their Chinese counterparts and also to enable them to take some concrete steps in the matter, but they were not permitted to visit the site. Many Indians assumed this action of the People's Republic of China to be improper, especially, when the People's Republic of China again tried to raise the slogan of ***Hindi-Chini Bhai-Bhai*** [Indians and Chinese are brothers], talked of resolving all its disputes not only with India but also with others through the policy of accommodation and showed willingness to do business with them.

Similarly, Indian people-general and particular- both did not like the publication of maps by two magazines in September 2004 in which Sikkim was shown as the separate nation. Many in the academic and educational fields considered it such a mischievous act of which the Government of the People's Republic of China cannot absolve itself. They rightly argued that the People's Republic of China was under the Communist rule where no publication was carried out without the consent of the Government. Then, how could it be possible that some magazines published such type of maps? It was a clear indication of Beijing's withdrawal from the commitment it made during Atal Behari Vajpayee's visit to the City in 2002.

In fact, both the above acts showed frustration of the People's Republic of China and indicated its old policy of breaking word; it created confusion in minds for which the Iron man as well as the maker of United India, Sardar Vallabhbhai Patel had cautioned his countrymen. In this regard, particularly disagreeing with his comrade colleague and the first Prime Minister, Pt. Jawaharlal Nehru, he suggested the latter to make his stand clear with regard to relations with China. In his letter written to Nehru on November 26, 1949, Patel advised: ***"We must have a clear idea."*** In failing to do so, Sardar Patel added further: ***"We should remember that the Chinese and their source of inspiration would not miss any opportunity of exploiting any of our weak points, partly in support of their ambitions."*** And then in the year 1962, as the whole world knows, the extent of warning of Sardar Vallabhbhai Patel was justified.

The extent of frustration of the People's Republic of China could be imagined from its urge to the Information and Broadcasting Ministry in New Delhi and through its Consulate in Mumbai to the organizers to take necessary action so that a film, based on the life of Dalai Lama, was pulled out of the Third Eye Asian Film Festival held in Mumbai [Bombay] between 21 and 28 August 2004.

Frustration and a policy of breaking word, again and again, can never create an atmosphere of trust. If the People's Republic of China is sincere to go ahead for co-operation and to do business or if it is serious about resolving all disputes with India, or to settle problems with other nations like Taiwan or Tibet, it has to create atmosphere of trust coming out of frustration and by giving up the policy of breaking word by taking some productive steps. It is absolutely necessary. No nation of the world can make fool, time and again, the people of another country in these days of mass awakening by adopting double standard. Also, merely some liberal steps taken to serve the purpose on particular occasions or showing flexibilities are not enough in this regard. Beijing has to understand it. If it fails to do so, no productive or welfaristic results even from continuous dialogues can be feasible.

Index